THE GHOSTS OF VERSAILLES

A Grand Opera Buffa in Two Acts

Suggested by *La Mère coupable* of Pierre-Augustin Caron de Beaumarchais

Music by John Corigliano

Libretto by William M. Hoffman

Commissioned by the Metropolitan Opera Company for its 100th anniversary

G. SCHIRMER, *Inc.*

DISTRIBUTED BY

HAL•LEONARD®
CORPORATION

7777 W. BLUEMOUND RD. P.O. BOX 13819 MILWAUKEE, WI 53213

CONTENTS

CHARACTERS

(in order of appearance)

Ghosts

WOMAN WITH HAT, elegant woman in her thirties .... Mezzo-soprano

LOUIS XVI, slow, self-important, in his late thirties .... Bass

MARQUIS, Louis's young confidant, a dandy .... Tenor

TRIO OF GOSSIPS .... Soprano, Soprano, Alto

OPERA QUARTET, jaded aristocrats .... Soprano, Alto, Tenor, Bass

PIERRE-AUGUSTIN CARON DE BEAUMARCHAIS, author of *The Barber of Seville*
and *The Marriage of Figaro*, passionate, quick, middle-aged .... Bass-baritone

MARIE ANTOINETTE, soulfully beautiful, vulnerable, warm, yet willful,
in her thirties .... Soprano

Players

FIGARO, Count Almaviva's wily servant, middle-aged .... Baritone

SUSANNA, Figaro's loyal but independent wife, middle-aged .... Soprano

COUNT ALMAVIVA, a proud, stubborn Spanish aristocrat, middle-aged .... Tenor

ROSINA, his still-beautiful, grieving wife, in her forties .... Soprano

LEON, Rosina's son by Cherubino, about twenty .... Tenor

FLORESTINE, Almaviva's daughter, about twenty .... Coloratura soprano

PATRICK HONORE BEGEARSS, Almaviva's treacherous friend, middle-aged .... Tenor

WILHELM, doltish young servant of Bégearss .... Speaking part

CHERUBINO, a former page of Almaviva, handsome, in his late teens .... Mezzo-soprano

SULEYMAN PASHA, Turkish ambassador, heavy, bald, middle-aged or older .... Bass

BRITISH AMBASSADOR, distinguished older gentleman .... Baritone

SAMIRA, sultry Egyptian singer .... Mezzo-soprano

DUCHESS (living version of Woman with Hat) .... Mezzo-soprano
(sung by WOMAN WITH HAT)

LIVING MARIE ANTOINETTE, careworn figure of David's portrait,
humbled by great suffering .... Soprano
(sung by ghost MARIE ANTOINETTE)

Others: pursuers of Figaro, Turkish duelists, page, dancing and harem girls, "rheita" players,
acrobats, revolutionary guards, revolutionary women, courtiers, dancers, prison guards,
prisoners, soldiers.

TIME: The present and the autumn of 1793.

PLACE: Marie Antoinette's theater in the Petit Trianon, Versailles.

PRODUCTION NOTE

The basic premise of *The Ghosts of Versailles* is that a group of ghosts is watching an opera. Because of this structure the opera takes place on three planes of reality:

1) The world of eternity, inhabited by ghosts

2) The world of the stage, peopled by dramatic characters

3) The world of history, populated by mortals

Our opera begins in the ghost world, which is the most fantastic and the most contemporary. It enters the stage world when the spectral playwright Beaumarchais raises the curtain on *A Figaro for Antonia,* the buffa-within-the-opera that he has written to amuse Marie Antoinette two hundred years after their deaths.

The ghostly characters watching the onstage production are fantasy creatures themselves. If the makeup or costumes of the onstage characters outdo those of the ghosts, or if the sets are too ambiguous or surrealistic, it will be difficult for the audience to distinguish among the worlds. *Therefore, the production on the stage-within-a-stage should almost always be more realistic than the ghost world.*

The ghost and the stage worlds are distinct until the second scene of Act 2, when Beaumarchais enters the opera-within-the-opera and Figaro is summoned by Marie Antoinette to the afterworld. At that point the two worlds blend and we enter a third realm: the historical (or objective) universe of the Paris streets, the Almaviva ballroom, and the Place de la Révolution. The scenic design of this last world should be grand operatic: representational sets, realistic costumes.

The Ghosts of Versailles represents a journey from the most fantastic to the most realistic. In the last scene, however, all three planes are juxtaposed: the historical Marie Antoinette is executed in the Place de la Révolution, the cast of *A Figaro for Antonia* makes their escape to London in a balloon, and the ghosts of the queen and Beaumarchais walk off together into the land of eternal delight—the gardens of Aguas Frescas.

—W.M.H.

to Anthony Holland, friend and collaborator

May memory restore again and again
The smallest color of the smallest day:
Time is the school in which we learn,
Time is the fire in which we burn.

—DELMORE SCHWARTZ

Acknowledgments

Special thanks to Osama A. Abusitta, John Atkins, Bob Campbell, Colin Graham, Joel Honig, Sandy Kadet, El-azza M'Hammed, Ross MacLean, Michael Mace, James McCourt, Steven Mercurio, Darragh Park, Philip Ramey, Sheldon Shkolnik, Mark Thalenberg, Denise Ulban, Kalman Ullmann, Jean-Claude van Itallie, Serapio Walton, and MaryAnn Wrobleski for their help and patience. I am grateful to the National Endowment for the Arts for a librettist grant and to the Circle Repertory Company for their support.

Credit is due for the lines from "Calmly We Walk Through This April's Day," by Delmore Schwartz (from *Selected Poems: Summer Knowledge*. Copyright © 1959 by Delmore Schwartz. Reprinted by permission of New Directions Publishing Company).

Synopsis

Act I, Prologue: The curtain rises on a world populated by the ghosts of the courtiers of Louis XVI of France. They have gathered to hear a performance of the new opera by the ghost of Pierre-Augustin Caron de Beaumarchais, author of the plays *The Barber of Seville* and *The Marriage of Figaro.* Marie Antoinette's private theater at the Petit Trianon in Versailles is reconstructed before our eyes, and several events occur in a dreamlike sequence: the Woman With Hat descends to the stage in an armchair while singing a musical excerpt from the play *The Marriage of Figaro;* the ghosts of Louis XVI and his confidant, the Marquis, play cards and discuss the queen, who is being courted by a commoner, Beaumarchais; three women gossip that the ghost of Beaumarchais is in love with the ghost of Marie Antoinette; an orchestra gathers onstage for the performance of Beaumarchais's opera and tunes up; and the ghosts of four jaded aristocrats arrive for the performance.

The ghosts of Beaumarchais and Marie Antoinette enter. He serenades her, even though he knows she cannot love him. Marie Antoinette has not found peace in death; after two hundred years she still grieves for her lost life. Terrifying images of her execution day haunt her *(Aria).* Beaumarchais resourcefully offers to cure the queen's melancholy through a performance of his new opera, *A Figaro for Antonia,* which features the latest exploits of Figaro and the Almaviva family. He signals for a preview of the opera to begin.

The curtains of Marie Antoinette's theater open to reveal the elegant drawing room of the Almaviva mansion. Figaro, Count Almaviva's obviously harried servant, now middle-aged, cautiously enters the seemingly unoccupied room; numerous people suddenly emerge from hiding places and chase him. After trapping his pursuers in a tiny closet, Figaro gloats over their jealousy of his varied career *(Aria).* Beaumarchais ends the preview just as Figaro's pursuers break out of the locked closet.

All of the ghosts are delighted with the opera, except for Marie Antoinette, who is saddened by its evocation of life. Moved by compassion, Beaumarchais offers to bring Marie Antoinette back to life; through the magic power of his words and music, he will use her diamond necklace to change the course of history and save her from death in the French Revolution. Marie Antoinette warns Beaumarchais that this might endanger his immortal soul, but he refuses to listen. He uses her necklace as a charm to begin the performance of his opera.

Act I, Scene 1: *A Figaro for Antonia* is set in Paris during the autumn of 1793, the beginning of the Reign of Terror; Louis XVI has been executed, Marie Antoinette is imprisoned and condemned to death, and the Almaviva family has settled in France after escaping revolution in Spain. Marie Antoinette's diamond necklace is being safeguarded by her old friend, Count Almaviva, the Spanish ambassador. He intends to sell it for a million pounds to the British ambassador at a diplomatic reception that night at the Turkish embassy; with the proceeds, he will secure Marie Antoinette's freedom and smuggle her to safety in the New World.

Beaumarchais interrupts the performance of his opera to outline its exposition to the ghosts. Life has not been kind to Rosina, the Countess Almaviva, in the twenty years since the conclusion of *The Marriage of Figaro*. She has had a son by Cherubino, the Count's former page, and, consequently, her husband has become cold and distant to her. Ironically, Rosina's son, Léon, has fallen in love with Florestine, Count Almaviva's illegitimate daughter. But the Count has never been able to forgive his wife's infidelity, and so he has refused to give his consent to Léon's marriage to Florestine. Instead, he has offered his daughter's hand to his best friend, Patrick Honoré Bégearss, who, unbeknownst to Almaviva, is a spy for the revolutionaries.

The performance of Beaumarchais's opera continues. Figaro and his wife, Susanna, arrive ostensibly to clean the Count's quarters, but actually to search them. Susanna finds Marie Antoinette's diamonds in Almaviva's pocket, and she and Figaro inquire as to how he obtained the jewels. They try to warn him about Bégearss' traitorous activities, but the Count simply dismisses Figaro for insubordination. Almaviva leaves.

Susanna and Figaro hide when Bégearss and his doltish servant Wilhelm unexpectedly enter the room. Bégearss cruelly beats Wilhelm for forgetting where Almaviva plans to sell Marie Antoinette's necklace; he has thereby foiled Bégearss' scheme to expose the Count's plot to save the queen. Bégearss reveals his secret intentions: to capture the queen's jewels and keep them for himself, execute Almaviva, make Rosina and Léon his servants, and marry Florestine. After having a vision of Florestine declaring her love for Léon, Bégearss' resolve intensifies and he boasts of his wickedness *(Aria)*. Suddenly Wilhelm remembers where Almaviva plans to sell the jewels. Susanna and Figaro sneak out to attempt to save the Count from treachery.

Act I, Scene 2: Feeling empathy for young Florestine's plight in the opera, Marie Antoinette reminisces with Beaumarchais about her own arrival in France, at the age of fifteen. But when Beaumarchais alludes to Marie Antoinette's future— alone with him, he hopes, in the New World—Louis becomes furious with jealousy. Beaumarchais quickly begins another scene of his opera to diffuse the tension.

Act I, Scene 3: In Rosina's boudoir, Bégearss hypocritically implores Almaviva to forgive the Countess' infidelity, but the Count remains merciless. Rosina nostalgically recalls her affair with Cherubino, twenty years ago in Seville; in a flashback, we see the lovers having a tryst in the garden of Aguas Frescas *(Duet)*. Much to Louis's discomfort, Beaumarchais and Marie Antoinette become more intimate as they watch the opera, and they join in song with the onstage lovers *(Quartet)*. But just as Beaumarchais and Marie Antoinette, inspired by the stage action, are about to kiss, Louis stops them by placing his sword between their lips.

Act I, Scene 4: Protesting that Beaumarchais is using his opera to steal his wife, Louis challenges the playwright to a duel. The other ghosts are delighted by their antics *(Dueling song)*. But when Louis stabs Beaumarchais, the playwright pulls out the sword and returns it to the king. All dissolve in laughter—the ghosts cannot be injured, as they are already dead! Beaumarchais likewise attacks the king with his sword, and all the ghosts proceed to stab each other gleefully.

Act I, Scene 5: The performance of *A Figaro for Antonia* resumes. At a diplomatic reception at the Turkish embassy, Count Almaviva anxiously awaits the arrival of the British ambassador, to whom he hopes to sell Marie Antoinette's diamond necklace. The Turkish emissary, Suleyman Pasha, greets his guests and signals for the evening's entertainment to begin.

As Léon declares his love for Florestine, Rosina and Susanna warn Almaviva not to sell the jewels that evening. Bégearss enters with Wilhelm and a group of revolutionary guards disguised as diplomats; they plan to capture the Count when he sells the diamonds. Finally, the British ambassador arrives, and he and Almaviva retreat for a private conversation. But just as the ambassadors are about to exchange the jewels, they realize that they are being watched. The Pasha quickly remedies this embarrassing situation by calling upon the sultry Egyptian singer Samira to perform *(Cavatina* and *Cabaletta);* as part of her act, she brings on a group of dancing girls, one of whom is Figaro in disguise.

Later, the ambassadors again try to sneak off. This time, their exchange is interrupted by Figaro, still disguised as a dancing girl, who seductively offers them fruit while searching Almaviva's pockets for the diamonds. But when Figaro finally finds and takes the necklace, Wilhelm sees the theft and shouts for the guards. In a vain attempt to retrieve the jewels, Almaviva inadvertently snatches the wig from Figaro's head and reveals his true identity.

A chaotic chase breaks out, with the guests either trying to help Figaro or apprehend him. At the height of the frenzy, Figaro accidentally pulls open the curtain of the embassy's little stage, and a band of rheita (North African oboe) players, waiting to make their entrance as part of the evening's entertainment, marches out. As the Pasha desperately tries to restore order, Figaro leaps off the embassy's balcony to freedom.

Act II, Scene 1: The ghosts slowly return to their seats after intermission for the beginning of the second act of *A Figaro for Antonia.* Beaumarchais reassures Marie Antoinette that he can change the course of history through the power of his art, and so bring her back to life. Again she warns him that in doing so he might risk his immortality, but he replies that he only wants to make her happy.

In Beaumarchais's opera, Figaro returns home, still in possession of the jewels, the morning after the diplomatic reception at the Turkish embassy. But, inexplicably, he refuses to give the necklace back to Almaviva—as Beaumarchais's script stipulates—and help the Count rescue Marie Antoinette from prison. Figaro thinks the queen is an arrogant traitor; he wants to keep the jewels and instead save Almaviva's family.

Furious at this rebellion by one of his characters, Beaumarchais stops the opera's performance. He frantically tries to convince the offended Marie Antoinette of his noble intentions *(Aria),* and then resolves to enter his own opera in order to force Figaro to follow the plot.

Act II, Scene 2: The performance of *A Figaro for Antonia* resumes at the point at which Beaumarchais had stopped the action. Almaviva threatens to banish Susanna if she cannot find Figaro, who has defiantly fled. He then urges his family to prepare for the ball they are hosting that evening; with the country's political unrest, it may be the last time the aristocrats can gather together. Susanna and Rosina comfort each other and lament the difficulties of their marriages *(Duet)*.

Suddenly, Figaro crawls in through the window, pursued by Beaumarchais, who tries to frighten and then intimidate him into returning the stolen necklace. Marie Antoinette summons Figaro, and Beaumarchais uses his magical powers to transport Figaro and Susanna to the ghost world. *(Interlude—"Journey to Limbo")*

Act II, Scene 3: Marie Antoinette awaits Figaro at the Temple of Love in the ghost world; she hopes to prove her innocence to him so that he will return the necklace. Nevertheless, Figaro accuses her of malevolence, so, at Marie Antoinette's behest, Beaumarchais conjures up a vision of her grossly unjust trial before the Revolutionary Tribunal, in which she is sentenced to death by the bloodthirsty citizens. As a result, Figaro begs forgiveness from the queen and pledges his help.

Act II, Scene 4: Beaumarchais sends Figaro and Susanna back to 1793; they suddenly find themselves in Paris on a street mobbed with violent women revolutionaries. Bégearss, the group's power-hungry leader, exhorts them to kill the aristocrats at Almaviva's party that evening *(Aria with Chorus)*.

Act II, Scene 5: At Almaviva's mansion, the remaining peers of Paris—those who have not yet fled, been imprisoned, or executed—gather one last time for a ball. Three ghosts haunt the party. Although the Count has banished him from the house, Léon sneaks in to see Florestine; their reminiscences of their love and courtship are echoed by those of Rosina and Almaviva *(Quartet)*.

Suddenly, Bégearss, with his followers, breaks in to arrest the aristocrats. He demands Marie Antoinette's diamonds from Almaviva, and threatens to torture him when he claims not to have them. Figaro steps forward to give the necklace to Bégearss, who takes it in the name of the French people. The villain then asks for Florestine's hand in marriage; when the Count denies his request, he threatens at first to kill Almaviva's family, but then orders them imprisoned.

Figaro implores Beaumarchais to use his magical powers to free them. But, as the queen had warned, the playwright's attempts to change history have cost him his powers. Susanna suddenly emerges from a hiding place and falsely accuses Wilhelm of impregnating her. This ruse sufficiently distracts the guards so that Figaro and Beaumarchais can escape; Susanna, however, is captured. After all have left the mansion, the ghosts dance. Finally, Marie Antoinette begins to realize the depth of Beaumarchais's love for her. *(Interlude)*

Act II, Scene 6: At the Conciergerie prison, terrified aristocrats await execution. The Almaviva household is ushered to a cell during the night by Wilhelm, who smugly makes advances toward Rosina. Almaviva rushes to her defense, and then begs forgiveness from his family for his arrogance and pride. Their prayers are joined with Marie Antoinette's petitions from her upstairs cell *(Quintet and Miserere)*.

At sunrise, two ominous-looking men enter the Almavivas' cell and tell the Count to prepare for death. But they quickly remove their disguises and reveal their identities—Figaro and Beaumarchais have come to help the Almaviva household escape! Susanna steals the key to Marie Antoinette's cell from Wilhelm by shrewdly preying upon his weakness for women. Almaviva runs to free the queen, but he is captured by Bégearss, who reiterates his demand to marry Florestine. This time, however, Figaro denounces Bégearss, in the name of the revolution, for possessing the queen's jewels. When Bégearss is furthermore accused of being a spy and counterrevolutionary, he and Wilhelm are seized and taken to the guillotine.

In the confusion, Beaumarchais retrieves Marie Antoinette's necklace, and Figaro begins to lead the Count's family to freedom. Almaviva hesitates to leave the prison before he can free the queen, so Beaumarchais takes from him the keys to Marie Antoinette's cell.

After all have fled, Beaumarchais prepares to free Marie Antoinette. But just as he is about to rescue her, the ghost of Marie Antoinette voices her desire that history be allowed to continue as it was *(Aria)*. She rejects "salvation"—she has fallen in love with Beaumarchais and wants to remain with him. The imprisoned queen is led away to execution; the ghosts of Beaumarchais and Marie Antoinette stay together.

Act II, Finale: At the Place de la Révolution, large crowds have gathered to witness the queen's execution. As the ghosts of Beaumarchais and Marie Antoinette slowly walk together to the distant gardens of Aguas Frescas, the historical Marie Antoinette is beheaded. Simultaneously, the Almaviva household departs for the New World in a Montgolfier balloon. The execution site fades away, and Beaumarchais and Marie Antoinette reach Aguas Frescas, where they are met by the other ghosts. Beaumarchais places the jewels around Marie Antoinette's neck, and the two are united for eternity.

—MARY LOU HUMPHREY
G. SCHIRMER, INC.

ACT I

PROLOGUE

(The curtain rises, revealing a vast expanse of empty stage dimly lit and painted a friendly, glowing off-white. We see, randomly placed, pieces of Marie Antoinette's intimate private theater at the Petit Trianon in Versailles: a pillar or two, a chair, a box, the front curtain. The rest of the theater will slowly assemble itself before our eyes.

The beginning of the Prologue is also marked by the slow descent of an elegant woman, seated in a comfortable fauteuil, from above the proscenium arch to the stage. She is wearing an extremely large dress and vast hat depicting peace and plenty in the land of France. She sings Beaumarchais's words in The Marriage of Figaro *to the traditional tune "Marlbrough s'en va-t-en guerre" ["For He's a Jolly Good Fellow"].*

The following five sections of the Prologue—the descent of the Woman with Hat, the gossiping women, the card game between Louis XVI and the Marquis, the quartet of bored ghosts in the opera box, and the warm-up of the onstage orchestra—form a collage of events that start, stop, overlap, and intertwine.)

WOMAN WITH HAT

Mon coursier hors d'haleine,	[With my charger out of breath,
(Que mon cœur, mon cœur a de peine!)	(Alas, how weary is my heart!)
J'errais de plaine en plaine,	I wandered from field to field
Au gré du destrier.	At the whim of my steed.
Au gré du destrier	At the whim of my steed,
Sans varlet, n'écuyer,	Without page or squire,
Là près d'une fontaine,	Close by a fountain,
(Que mon cœur, mon cœur a de peine!)	(Alas, how weary is my heart!)
Songeant à ma Marraine,	Thinking about my girl,
Sentais mes pleurs couler. . .	I felt my tears fall.]

(Weird, silent dancing shapes appear in odd corners of the stage. A larger piece of the theater set and two men playing cards at a small table arrive onstage. The men consider which cards to play.)

WOMAN WITH HAT (continued)

Mon coursier hors d'haleine,
  (Que mon cœur, mon cœur a de peine!)
J'errais de plaine en plaine,
Au gré du destrier. . .
(Etc.)

LOUIS

(Collecting two cards)
My trick. Thank you, my friend.

MARQUIS

(Referring to card on table)
The queen languishes in despair, Your Majesty.

(Placing card on table.)

MARQUIS (continued)
Hopeless, afraid, she clings to the past.

LOUIS
(Placing card on top of the Marquis's)
A commoner is courting her.

MARQUIS
(Placing card on top of Louis's)
But will he have her?

LOUIS
(Furiously throwing down cards)
I don't care! Let him have her! Let him have her! I don't care!

(The Marquis collects the cards. They continue playing.)

(Three elegantly dressed women skitter in from the back like insects. The first carries a parasol. The other two wear knickers under flouncy dresses. They are mindlessly gossiping and find each other hilarious. The Woman with Hat disappears at this point.)

SECOND WOMAN
He's in love, he's in love, he's in love!

THIRD WOMAN
Beaumarchais's in love.

FIRST WOMAN
He's in love with Marie Antoinette.

(They laugh.)

ALL THREE WOMEN
The queen is sad. . . She longs for death. . . She's been dead for two hundred years!

THIRD WOMAN
She regrets her past.

SECOND WOMAN
She will not rest.

FIRST WOMAN
She seeks solace.

THIRD WOMAN
She can't find peace.

FIRST & SECOND WOMEN
She longs for death.

MARQUIS
The queen languishes in despair, Your Majesty.

LOUIS
I don't care. . .

ALL THREE WOMEN
She's been dead for two hundred years!
(They laugh.)

SECOND WOMAN
He's in love, he's in love, he's in
love!. . .

*(The women repeat then fade out as
they exit into the shadows.)*

LOUIS
Don't care. . . Don't care. . . Don't
care. . .

*(Enter a small onstage orchestra. The
players remove their instruments from
their cases, place their music on stands,
and tune up.)*

WOMAN WITH HAT
(Returning)
Mon coursier hors d'haleine,
     (Que mon cœur, mon cœur a de
     peine!)
J'errais de plaine en plaine,
Au gré du destrier.
(Etc.)

*(On one side of the stage-within-a-stage
an opera box rises into the air. A quartet of ghosts is in it.)*

FIRST WOMAN IN BOX
Another evening at the opera.

FIRST MAN IN BOX
I'm so bored.

SECOND WOMAN IN BOX
I'm so bored.

SECOND MAN IN BOX
Perhaps Beaumarchais can amuse us.

(The Woman with Hat exits.)

FIRST MAN IN BOX
Bored as a rug.

FIRST WOMAN IN BOX
(To Second Man in Box)
Well, I know you can't.

SECOND WOMAN IN BOX
Bored as an egg.

SECOND MAN IN BOX
(To First Woman in Box)
Oh, Lucienne, how you bore me.

FIRST MAN IN BOX
Bored as a potato.

FIRST WOMAN IN BOX
I loathe you.

SECOND MAN IN BOX
I'm so bored.

SECOND WOMAN IN BOX
Rug.

FIRST MAN IN BOX
Egg.

FIRST WOMAN IN BOX
Bored as an egg.

SECOND WOMAN IN BOX
Potato.

FIRST MAN IN BOX
Rug.

SECOND MAN IN BOX
Bored.

FIRST MAN IN BOX
Another evening at the opera.

SECOND WOMAN IN BOX
Perhaps Beaumarchais can amuse us.

FIRST MAN IN BOX
(To Second Woman in Box)
Well, I know you can't.

SECOND MAN IN BOX
Oh, how you bore me.

FIRST WOMAN IN BOX
I'm so bored.

SECOND WOMAN IN BOX
I loathe you.

FIRST MAN IN BOX
I'm so bored.

SECOND MAN IN BOX
I'm so bored.

SECOND WOMAN IN BOX
Oh, so bored.

(The Three Women reenter.)

SECOND WOMAN
He's in love, he's in love, he's in love!

THIRD WOMAN
Beaumarchais's in love.
(Etc.)

WOMAN WITH HAT
(Returning)
. . . d'ha . . . lei . . . ne . . .
(Etc.)

FIRST MAN IN BOX

Bored.

ALL

Bored.

(They yawn and repeat "bored" till the end of this section.)

MARQUIS

The queen languishes in despair, Your Majesty.

LOUIS

I don't care, I don't care.

MARQUIS

Hopeless, afraid, she clings to the past.

WOMAN WITH HAT

. . . Au . . . gré . . . du . . . destrier
(Etc.)

LOUIS

A commoner is courting her.

MARQUIS

But will he have her?

(The Three Women race in and out of vision.)

LOUIS

I don't care, I don't care. No! I don't! I don't care! Don't! No! Don't care!

THREE WOMEN

He's in love. . .
(Etc.)

(Etc. ad lib.)

MARQUIS

But will he have her?

(Etc. ad lib.)

(When the theater set is almost complete, a light appears upstage in the distance. As it gradually moves forward and grows in intensity, silencing the restless, angry ghosts, we see that it consists of two shimmering figures, Marie Antoinette and Beaumarchais. Beaumarchais is serenading the queen, who reclines, ignoring him. The court bows to her.

Marie Antoinette is wearing a simple white dress and straw hat. She seems to be in her thirties, at the height of her beauty. Beaumarchais appears to be middle-aged. He is brilliant, quick, worldly, and deliberately negligent about his clothing.)

BEAUMARCHAIS

All-powerful Queen of Beauty
And ruler of my willing heart,
To make you smile is my duty,
To make you laugh is all my art.

MARIE ANTOINETTE

Is there no escape from you, Beaumarchais? Why do you persecute me with your love?

BEAUMARCHAIS

Coldly denying,
Boldly declining,
Grieving, deceiving,
She lies when she tells me
She'd like to expel me
And cares for me not.

MARIE ANTOINETTE

I no longer long to love. Leave me in peace, Beaumarchais. As colors fade from flowers, feelings leave the soul.

(He follows her.)

BEAUMARCHAIS

Orion, Orion,
Even the moon moves
And is laced gently by leaves.

ARIA

MARIE ANTOINETTE

They are always with me:
The unbounded waiting,
The odor of blood on steel,
The terrible sound.

They are always with me:
The crying children,
The crowds dancing,
Severed heads on pikes.
Fear, terror, panic—
Lord, let me forget!

> Once there was a golden bird
> In a garden of silver trees.
> From the courtyard could be heard
> The laughter of women at their ease.

They are always with me:
The breaking windows,
The throngs pushing,
Hawking souvenirs,
Stuffing food into jeering mouths
That foam with wine;
A screaming horse;
A man mounting a girl—

A party, a fair, a picnic—
Lord, Lord, let me forget,
Let me forget!

MARIE ANTOINETTE (continued)

Once there was a golden bird
In a garden of silver trees.
From the courtyard could be heard
The laughter of women at their ease.

It is time:
Eleven o'clock.
"What will you eat?" they ask.
"You will wear white," they say.
They cut my hair.
They give me back my ring.
Am I going to my wedding?

The back of an oxcart in the October sun.
The people insult me, scorn me,
They spit at me as I pass.
What are those flames?
Flags in the streets of Saint Honoré.
What is that noise?
My funeral drums.

I climb the stairs.
Am I dreaming?
Someone wake me!
Three steps. Four.
I want to cry out,
"I am good!
I am innocent!"
Seven. Eight.
"Take care of my children!"
Nine. Ten.
"Don't take me!
Don't take me!"
Lord, let me forget!
Grant me oblivion!

LOUIS

My wife was always hard to please . . . You must change, Antonia, with the times. We are dead! It is time to rejoice!

GHOSTS

Bored. . . Dead. . . Rug. . . Potato. . . It's time to rejoice!

LOUIS

(Stopping them with a withering stare)
Beaumarchais, you promised us an opera.

BEAUMARCHAIS

Only if Her Majesty desires it.

LOUIS

To please us, Antonia?

GHOSTS

(To Marie Antoinette, like spoiled children to their mother)
Please us. . . Rug. . . Egg. . . Bored. . . It's time rejoice!

(Louis glares murderously at ghosts.)

LOUIS

Really!

(Marie Antoinette looks on impassively, dabbing the tears at the corners of her eyes.)

BEAUMARCHAIS

(To Marie Antoinette)
I am a doctor, Your Majesty. My opera can cure melancholy. My words are a spell. Listen to my title: *A Figaro. . .*

GHOSTS

Figaro?. . . A Figaro?. . .

BEAUMARCHAIS

. . . for Antonia.

GHOSTS

(With a sense of wonder)
. . . Oooh. . . *for Antonia. . . Ah. . . Figaro. . .*

BEAUMARCHAIS

Watch! Here's a sample.

(Beaumarchais claps his hands. The Overture to the opera-within-the-opera begins, and the curtains of the little stage fly open. We see the drawing room of the Almaviva mansion in Paris at the start of the Reign of Terror, in the autumn of 1793. It is an elegant chamber with many doors—one leading to a closet—sofas, chairs, screens, a large chest, a big window, and a barber's chair with its back to the audience. One of the doors opens. Figaro peeks into the room, making sure that it is unoccupied. He enters carefully, quietly, mopping his brow—obviously he has been running. He looks around slowly, makes his way warily to an armchair, and is about to sit down when a group of pursuers leaps out from behind the screens and furniture and rushes in through the doors.)

PURSUERS*

There's Figaro!

FIGARO

Oh, no! Here we go again!

PURSUERS

Stop!

(Figaro opens one of the doors. He is about to leave when he is blocked by bearded Muscovite traders.)

TRADERS

He owes me money!

PURSUERS

Stop!

---

*   Note: the shaded material takes places on the stage-within-a-stage.

(Figaro runs to the window. He is about to climb out but is thwarted by an old man on a ladder who leans in the window.)

MAN ON LADDER

You thief, you stole my daughter!

(He is echoed by a man inside the room.)

MAN IN ROOM

... my wife!

(Figaro runs toward the screens but is stopped by Susanna, who steps from behind holding a rolling pin.)

FIGARO

My wife!

SUSANNA

You'll pay! You'll pay! You'll pay!

(Figaro runs to the other side of the stage.)

PURSUERS

Stop! Stop, Figaro!

(He tries to hide in the barber's chair, turning it around as he does so, revealing a man with lather on his face.)

FIGARO

Oops!

MAN WITH LATHER

Figaro! How could you leave me like this?

(Pursued by women with children, Figaro runs behind the sofa.)

WOMAN HOLDING INFANT

Figaro! Look at your son. Give him a kiss.

OTHER WOMEN HOLDING CHILDREN

Where are you, Figaro? Come to me, Figaro.

(Figaro pokes his head up from behind sofa.)

FIGARO

They love me! Just listen to them.
(Susanna approaches menacingly, hiding her rolling pin.)
Adorable!

SUSANNA

Where are you, Figaro? Come to me...

(She tries to hit Figaro, who ducks. Almaviva has now caught up to him and grabs him by the collar.)

ALMAVIVA

Wretch! Did you forget to deliver the letter?

FIGARO

No, Master, I swear it.

(Susanna marches toward them. Figaro breaks away and runs.)

SUSANNA

(Pointing to the children one by one)
Is that your child, is that your child?

FIGARO

I've never seen them before.

PURSUERS

Stop! Stop, Figaro!

(Figaro runs into the man with lather on his face.)

MAN WITH LATHER

Figaro, when will you finish my shave?

(Pursuers crowd around Figaro, who turns to respond to each question.)

TRADERS

Figaro, you owe us money.

ALMAVIVA

Figaro!

FIGARO

Yes, Sir.

ALMAVIVA

Did you forget to deliver the letter?

FIGARO

No, Sir.

SUSANNA

Figaro!

FIGARO

Yes, Mam.

SUSANNA	FIGARO
Figaro! Is that your child?	*(More and more frantically)*
	No, Mam. . . Yes, Sir. . . No, Sir. . .
	Yes, Sir. . . No, Mam. . . No, Sir. . .
	Yes, Mam. . . Yes. . . No. . . Mam. . .
ALMAVIVA	Sir. . . STOP!!
Figaro! Did you forget to deliver the let-ter?	

MAN WITH LATHER

Figaro! Finish my shave.

MAN ON LADDER

Figaro! You thief, you stole my daughter.

TRADERS

Figaro! You owe us money.

WOMAN HOLDING INFANT

Figaro! Give him a kiss.

OTHER WOMEN WITH CHILDREN
Figaro, Figaro, come to me, Figaro. . .
come to us, Figaro.

*(Stunned by Figaro's outburst, the pursuers allow him to dart away. The chase
resumes. Excited by the onstage melee, the ghosts initiate one of their own, in
which all of them except Marie Antoinette, Beaumarchais, Louis, the Marquis,
and the Woman with Hat participate. Madness has broken out, onstage and off.)*

PURSUERS
(Ad lib.)
Get 'im!. . . There he is!. . . Over here!. . . I see him!. . .

GHOSTS
Dead!. . . Egg!. . . Bored!. . . Potato!. . .

PURSUERS
Stop! Stop, Figaro!

PURSUERS & GHOSTS
Stop! Stop, Figaro!

*(Figaro leads his pursuers into a closet we know is too small for even one person.
The music grows softer as the onstage group grows smaller.)*

GHOSTS
Stop him, stop Figaro! . . .

SUSANNA
Stop him. . .

GHOSTS
Stop him, stop. . .

ALMAVIVA
Figaro!

*(The stage is empty. Figaro appears through another door, races toward the closet,
slams it shut, and locks the pursuers inside. They bang loudly, and he tosses the key
out the window.)*

ARIA

FIGARO
They wish they could kill me.
They wish they could stop me.
They hate me, they loathe me.
Tell me why do they torment me so.
(He smiles shyly.)
They're jealous!
Of what. . .
(He slams his hand against the door to stop the banging.)
. . . You may ask.

FIGARO (continued)

(He slumps down, imitating an old man.)
I pant when I walk.
I wheeze when I talk.
My muscles are slack.
I've a pain in my back.
I'm lazy by nature.
I'm also a lecher.
I'm proud, I'm greedy.
My manners are shoddy.
Of what then are they jealous?

BEAUMARCHAIS

I love that little fellow.

LOUIS

You love yourself.

FIGARO

Nothing. . .

MARIE ANTOINETTE

He's charming.
(Marie Antoinette smiles.)

BEAUMARCHAIS

She's smiling.

WOMAN WITH HAT

Adorable.

FIGARO

Except. . . .
They're jealous!. . . They're jealous!. . . Jealous!. . .
Of what, you may ask?
(He stoops again.)
My money is low.
My status less than quo.
I'm poor, I'm weak.
My future's rather bleak.
I'm stooped, I'm spent.
I'm almost impotent.

Once master, now valet,
As fortune would have it,
I've been diplomat, acrobat,
Teacher of etiquette,
Student and swordsman,
Spy and musician.
I've been satirist, pessimist,
Surgeon and Calvinist,
Spanish economist,

FIGARO (continued)

Clockmaker, pharmacist,
Veterinarian,
Egalitarian,
Heathen comedian,
Pious tragedian.

I've been orator, poet,
And pirate and prophet,
A man for the ladies
And father of babies,
Drunken and sober,
A husband and sailor,
Banker and brother
And barber and lover. . .
And now I'm a failure!

I've seen everything, done everything, had everything,. . . and lost everything.
Of what then are they jealous?

MARIE ANTOINETTE

Poor Figaro.

WOMAN WITH HAT

Poor man, poor man.

FIGARO

My spirit—
A vapor deliquescent,
An effervescent liquid
Pervading, invading, taking my body,
Making me fluid, light, buoyant.
I'm sunlight, a moonbeam,
And carefree I fly to the stars:

Capella, Carina,
Spica, Auriga,
Libra, Lyra,
Andromeda,
Fornax, Phoenix,
Bellatrix, Pollux.
Joy! Joy!
Carefree I fly to the stars:
Vulpecula, Vela,
Columba, Ara,
Lacerta,
Lupus, Lepus—
Joy! Joy! Joy!
Pegasus, Perseus, Aquila.
Joy! Joy! Joy!
Peg—
(The banging resumes, bringing Figaro back to reality.)

FIGARO (continued)

They wish they could kill me.
They wish they could stop me.
They hate me, they loathe me.
And we know why they must torment me so!
They're jealous! They're jealous! They're jealous!... Yes, jealous!
Of Figaro, your Figaro.
I'm back at last!

I've been veterinarian,
Egalitarian,
Heathen comedian,
Pious tragedian,
Orator, poet,
And pirate and prophet,
A man for the ladies
And father of babies,
Drunken and sober,
A husband and sailor,
Banker and brother
And barber and lover.
Diplomat, acrobat,
Teacher of etiquette, me!
Satirist, pessimist,
Surgeon and Calvinist,
I've been diplomat, acrobat,
Teacher of etiquette,
Student and swordsman,
Spy and musician,
Satirist, pessimist,
Surgeon and Calvinist,
Spanish economist,
Clockmaker, pharmacist.
I'm Figaro,
Your Figaro,
I'm home again,
Home again!

(The door flies open. The pursuers spill out onto the floor and look up at Figaro, who stares at them and freezes. Beaumarchais closes the curtain of the little stage as the ghosts applaud. Figaro takes a curtain call.)

(The ghosts are delighted, except Marie Antoinette, who weeps softly.)

LOUIS

Bravo, bravo, bravi!

MARQUIS

Brilliant, Beaumarchais.

BEAUMARCHAIS

Why are you weeping, Your Majesty?

MARIE ANTOINETTE

It was so beautiful, so full of life.

BEAUMARCHAIS

Antonia, I can bring you back to life, home again. . . May I borrow your necklace, Your Highness?

GHOSTS

(Whispering)
Necklace? . . . Her necklace?

MARIE ANTOINETTE

My necklace?

BEAUMARCHAIS

With your necklace I shall change your past. I shall show you history as it should have been.

MARIE ANTOINETTE

I want to live again.

BEAUMARCHAIS

I'll make you live again. I, Pierre-Augustin Caron de Beaumarchais, will change the course of history. . . with a necklace.

MARIE ANTOINETTE

You are mad. You could lose your immortal soul.

BEAUMARCHAIS

The Revolution never happens! There is no guillotine! A new age dawns! Marie Antoinette lives! Love me, Your Majesty!

MARIE ANTOINETTE

I cannot love.

LOUIS

(Sarcastically)
Believe her, Beaumarchais.

BEAUMARCHAIS

I have the powers of a god. Watch me!
(He pours the necklace from one hand to the other. Like a fortune teller:)
Diamonds. . . I see diamonds. . . I see a room with many doors. . . Diamonds. . . Doors. . . Magic!

(Beaumarchais turns his back to the audience and holds the diamonds aloft.)

SCENE 1

(Beaumarchais lowers his arms and the curtains open again. We see the same drawing room as before, but this time Count Almaviva is kneeling in the middle of it, frozen in position, holding aloft a diamond necklace identical to Beaumarchais's. Beaumarchais turns around. He no longer has the necklace. Through the window we see three soldiers marching around a square.)

BEAUMARCHAIS

It is Paris. . . the autumn of ninety-three. . . Terror. . . Revolution. . . The king is dead. The queen awaits her fate in prison.

MARIE ANTOINETTE

(A cry of pain)
Ah!

LOUIS

(Going to his wife's side)
Beaumarchais!

BEAUMARCHAIS

I can help her. Believe in me.
(To Marie Antoinette)
You have entrusted your diamonds to your old friend, the Spanish ambassador, Count Almaviva.

MARIE ANTOINETTE

Juan Carlo!

(Beaumarchais animates Almaviva with the gestures of an orchestra conductor.)

ALMAVIVA

O heavenly Father, hear my vow: On my life I promise to set free Thy persecuted daughter, Marie Antoinette of France. . .
(He bows his head.)

MARIE ANTOINETTE

(Crying out to Almaviva, who does not hear her)
Save me! Save me! I want to live!

LOUIS

(To Marie Antoinette)
Antonia!
(To Beaumarchais)
How can you be so cruel? You open old wounds.

ALMAVIVA

(Lifting his head)
. . . And if it be Thy will, O Lord, tonight I shall sell these jewels to the English ambassador. . .
(He lowers his head.)

MARIE ANTOINETTE

My youth! My love!

LOUIS

(To Beaumarchais)
Madman! Scoundrel!

ALMAVIVA

(Lifting his head)
At the reception of the Turkish Embassy. . .

LOUIS

(Putting his hands over his ears.)
Stop it! Stop it! *Stop it!*.

BEAUMARCHAIS

(Freezing Almaviva and the soldiers with a gesture)
I am a wizard. My logic is magic. . . Our cast of characters:
(He snaps his fingers.)
Rosina!—
(We see an apparition of Rosina high above the stage. She is seated in a chair, weeping.)
the wife of Count Almaviva in my first two operas. But life has not been kind to her. For the last twenty years her husband has been distant and cold because—how shall I put this delicately? Well, remember Almaviva's young page, Cherubino? He and Rosina had a child. . .
(Ghosts react with surprise.)
And here is that son—Léon.
(Léon appears in another location. The apparition of Rosina remains.)
Handsome lad, isn't he? Léon has fallen in love with. . .
(He snaps his fingers and Florestine appears at Léon's side. They look at each other lovingly.)
Florestine. She is the Count's offspring by. . .
(To Marie Antoinette)
You knew the woman, Your Highness.

MARIE ANTOINETTE

The Baroness of Oberkirch? The Countess of Noailles?

BEAUMARCHAIS

(Mysteriously)
A nameless woman of high rank.
(Marie Antoinette nods knowingly.)
Here's the problem: Almaviva has never forgiven his wife's infidelity, and Léon is a constant reminder of it. The Count refuses to give his consent to the marriage of his daughter to Rosina's son, even though the children are not related by blood, which you'll see if you've done your figuring correctly. Instead, Almaviva has promised his daughter to his best friend. . .
(Bégearss appears in a distant area of the stage.)
. . .our villain, Patrick Honoré Bégearss.
(With a wave of his hand Beaumarchais makes all the apparitions disappear, leaving Almaviva alone on stage.)
Of course, there are two more characters: Figaro, whom you've already met, and his wife, Susanna—

GHOSTS

Enough. . . Endless. . . What about the jewels?. . . Boring. . . I don't understand. . . Diamonds. . . Egg. . . Potato. . .

MARIE ANTOINETTE

It's simple: Rosina had a child by Cherubino, Almaviva by Madame X. The children, who are related only by marriage, fall in love. I understand that—but what about my jewels?

LOUIS

That's all she ever thinks about.

BEAUMARCHAIS

(Defensively to Marie Antoinette)
The plot is a little complicated. . . but it'll all work out. You'll see. I promise, Your Highness.

LOUIS

Get on with it, Beaumarchais!

LOUIS

I couldn't follow the last act of *The Marriage of Figaro* and this is even worse.

WOMAN WITH HAT

Her son is in love with *his* daughter. The father of her son is the count's former page, and the mother of his daughter is—

MARQUIS

No, because his father is not her father, and her mother is—

WOMAN WITH HAT

But they *have* to be related. Of course, they are. Then what they are doing is—

MARQUIS

No, no, no! You're getting it all mixed up. You see, Cherubino is not related to—

(They ad lib until cut off by Beaumarchais.)

(With an arcane gesture Beaumarchais reanimates Almaviva.)

ALMAVIVA

. . . And with the one million pounds, grant Her Majesty a safe refuge in the New World.
(He holds the necklace aloft.)
Ave Maria, gratia plena. Benedictus fructus ventris tuis . . .
(There is a loud knock at the door.)
Who is it?

FIGARO

Figaro.

SUSANNA

And Susanna.

ALMAVIVA

(Whispering, aside)
Those two. They mustn't see the jewels.
(He stuffs them into his pocket.)
One moment.

(He opens the door. Enter Figaro and Susanna with dusters, brooms, cloths, and mops.)

FIGARO

Just cleaning the room, Master.

SUSANNA

Tidy and clean, neat as a pin.

FIGARO

We won't be a minute.

(Figaro and Susanna quickly search the room while pretending to clean. Susanna spies the necklace hanging out of Almaviva's pocket and snatches it.)

SUSANNA

What's this?

ALMAVIVA

(Taking the necklace back)
None of your business.

FIGARO

Secrets from your loyal Figaro. . .

SUSANNA

And devoted Susanna?

ALMAVIVA

Devoted and loyal to Rosina and her son. I'll never forgive that woman.

SUSANNA

For the love of God, forgive your wife.

FIGARO

And forgive her son. Let him marry your daughter.

SUSANNA

My lady has already given her permission.

ALMAVIVA

How dare she! Florestine will marry Bégearss. He's the only man I trust.

SUSANNA

But, Master, he only pretends to be your friend.

ALMAVIVA

Mind your place.

FIGARO

He's a spy for the revolutionaries.

ALMAVIVA

Don't be absurd.

FIGARO

I caught his servant searching your room. . .

ALMAVIVA

I don't believe you.

FIGARO

. . . reading your letters.

ALMAVIVA

(Putting his hands over his ears)
I won't listen.

FIGARO

Where did you get that necklace?

ALMAVIVA

This time you've gone too far. . . I dismiss you, Figaro. Leave at once. You will obey! My wife will obey! I'm still king in this house!
(Exit Almaviva.)

LOUIS

I said the very same words.

SUSANNA

Stubborn! Oh, Figaro, what are we going to do? We'll starve.

FIGARO

(Tapping his head)
Not so long as I have this.

SUSANNA

What's this world coming to? Master sneaks around with stolen jewels; our mistress cries all day. And outside, Paris has gone mad: a king has lost his head, the queen languishes in jail. I am frightened for little folk like us.

FIGARO

Susanna, Susanna, at least we have each other.
(There are screams and blows offstage.)
But who is that coming?

SUSANNA

Bégearss and his servant Wilhelm. He is always beating him.

FIGARO

Miserable man. Let's hide and see what we can learn. Come, Susanna.
(They hide behind a screen as Bégearss enters beating Wilhelm.)

BEGEARSS

Fool! Idiot! Moron! You forgot where Almaviva plans to sell the jewels? How could you?

WILHELM

I read it in one of his letters, but then that Figaro came in and scared it right out of my mind.

BEGEARSS

When?!
(Kick)
Where?!
(Kick)
I need to know so I can expose the plot to save the queen. Think, you lunatic, think! Think! Think! Think! Think!

WILHELM
(Breaking down completely and groveling)
Uh. . . Uh. . . Uh. . . I can't. I'm sorry. I'm sorry I can't. I'm sorry I'm sorry I'm sorry I can't. . .

GHOSTS
Think. . . Can't. . . Lunatic. . . Hit 'em. . . Sorry. . .

MARIE ANTOINETTE
(Silencing ghosts)
Shhhhh!. . . Imbeciles!

(Beaumarchais offers her a cushion. She smiles at him and accepts it.)

WILHELM
Forgive me, Master, I beg you.

MARIE ANTOINETTE
Thank you, Beaumarchais.

WILHELM
What can I do?

BEGEARSS
What can you do? What can you do?. . . What you're good for: polish my boots. . . and keep thinking. . .

(Bégearss sits down and Wilhelm polishes his boots. Beaumarchais seats himself at the feet of Marie Antoinette. Bégearss smiles malevolently.)

RECITATIVE

I can't wait to betray Almaviva. . . When they arrest him I'll make him crawl to me on his hands and knees like a dog.
(Petting Wilhelm's head)
Good boy. . . But I'll send him to the scaffold anyway. And then I'll make the Countess my maid. Yes!
(He chuckles.)
And if she doesn't like that I'll send her to the cart also.
(He laughs.)
And Léon will be my page, as his father was to the Count. And Florestine, my wondrous Florestine, will be my mistress, my wife, my slave! Florestine will be my love. . . my love. . . my love. . .

(We see Florestine as in Bégearss' imagination. She is elevated, dressed in white, beautiful. She is rereading a letter she has just written, holding a quill in her hand.)

FLORESTINE
"Come to me, my love. I am yours, your mistress, your wife, your slave—totally, abjectly, passionately, savagely yours. Come to me, come to me, my love. Oh, Léon, Léon, Léon. . ."

BEGEARSS

Léon? Léon?! LEON?!

(He rises abruptly and kicks Wilhelm out of the way. The vision fades immediately.)

Dog! Out of my way! Out of my way!

(Shouting)

Léon and Florestine! Me! What about me—Patrick Honoré Bégearss? Scum!
It's true: I'm low, base, vile. But don't they know the king of beasts is the worm?

(During the following aria Wilhelm tries to remember the contents of the letter.)

ARIA OF THE WORM*

Oh, the lion may roar,
And the eagle may soar,
And man may sail the darkest sea,
But the worm lives on eternally.
Long live the worm.

Cut him in two,
Each part'll renew.
Slice him to bits,
The worm persists.
He still crawls on,
Scales walls on
Sheer will, and
Burrows burning sand.
Long live the worm.

He travels on by
The poor man's sty,
Groveling past
The royal palace,
And enters the coffin
Of the red-haired dauphin.
Long live the worm.

The wind whistles
And the storm bristles,
And mud covers the ground.
The worm wanders round and round
Morning and night,
Hidden from sight,
Over mountain and shore,
Wanting more and more,
Devouring city and plain,
Enduring snow and rain.
Long live the worm.

Oh, the lion dies,
The eagle dies,

---

* Suggested by Arrigo Boito's epic poem *Il Re Orso*.

BEGEARSS (continued)

And man dies. . .
(Maniacal laughter)

But the worm lives on eternally.
Long live the worm.

WILHELM

I remember, Master, I remember! The reception at the Turkish embassy! Tonight! Almaviva's going to sell the jewels to the English ambassador!
(Wilhelm grovels at Bégearss' feet and kisses them.)

BEGEARSS

Good boy. Good boy.
(Figaro and Susanna peek out from behind the screen.)

WILHELM

Thank you, Master, thank you.

SUSANNA

(Aside to Figaro)
We must warn the Count.

FIGARO

(Aside to Susanna)
He'll never believe us.

WILHELM

Or was it the Turkish ambassador at the English embassy? No, it was definitely
the Turkish embassy and the English—or was he Spanish—?

BEGEARSS

Enough! I know which one.

SUSANNA

What will we do? All is lost.

FIGARO

As long as I have my head I'll never give up. Come, Susanna, I have an idea.
(They sneak out.)

BEGEARSS

Ha! I have him now! Now I have them all! And Florestine will marry me—or
Doctor Guillotine! Come, Wilhelm.

(As they leave, the curtains close on the little stage.)

SCENE 2

GHOSTS

Rogue!. . . Villain!. . . Murderer!. . .

MARIE ANTOINETTE

That terrible man. Poor Florestine, I weep for her. She is so young. When I first came to France I was only fourteen.

BEAUMARCHAIS

It was May. There were parades in Lorraine. Remember?

MARIE ANTOINETTE

I remember I was frightened.

BEAUMARCHAIS

Ribbons in the trees of Compiègne. Remember?

MARIE ANTOINETTE

I remember I was lonely.

BEAUMARCHAIS

Fireworks at Versailles. Oh, how the people loved you.

MARIE ANTOINETTE

I was such a homesick little girl. . . Poor Florestine, don't let him marry her!

BEAUMARCHAIS

Don't be afraid, Your Majesty, I won't let that happen. And Almaviva and Figaro will foil Bégearss and bring you to the New World.
(She makes a disdainful face.)
And I'll be there to amuse you. Just the two of us.

LOUIS

The two of you? This time you go too far!
(His hand goes to his sword.)
I warned you. Defend yourself.

MARIE ANTOINETTE

(Putting her hand over her husband's)
Don't be absurd.

LOUIS

How dare he?

MARQUIS

Beaumarchais, do something!

(Marie Antoinette looks at Beaumarchais expectantly.)

BEAUMARCHAIS

(Leaping onto apron of little stage)
New scene: Rosina's boudoir.
(To Marie Antoinette as he opens the curtains)
They say New York is a lively town.

(He blows her a kiss. Louis stamps his foot.)

LOUIS

(To Marquis)
After all, she is my wife.

SCENE 3

(The curtain rises on the little stage. We are in Rosina's boudoir, with Rosina, Bégearss, and Almaviva. Beaumarchais leaves the apron.)

BEGEARSS

Turn the other cheek and forgive your wife, in the name of our friendship. I implore you.

ROSINA

Forgive me, I beg you, my husband.

ALMAVIVA

(Rigidly)
There's no mercy in my heart.

BEGEARSS

Forgive her, my friend.

ROSINA

Forgive me, my lord.

ALMAVIVA

(To Rosina)
I'll never relent.

BEGEARSS

(Aside)
His hatred fills me with joy.

ROSINA

If you loved me, let our children marry.

ALMAVIVA

I'd rather see them dead.

BEGEARSS

(Aside)
I'm in paradise.
(To Almaviva)
Forgive her, my friend.

ROSINA

And forgive our son.

ALMAVIVA

Neither! Never! You loved Cherubino. Now live with your shame.
(To Bégearss)
Come, my friend, let us discuss your wedding plans.

BEGEARSS

(To Rosina)
I did my best.

(Exit Bégearss and Almaviva.)

ROSINA

That man is a saint, but even he can't help me now. I am truly lost. Oh, Cherubino, I gave up my life for you.
(Sobbing)
Cherubino. . . Cherubino. . .

BEAUMARCHAIS

Now we go back in time, my friends. Let it be Spain, twenty years before. Let it be Seville, the full bloom of spring.

(Rosina's clothes fly off of her and she now is twenty years younger, dressed as a shepherdess. She puts on a blindfold. Meanwhile, the stage-within-a-stage has expanded to become a bower in the garden of Aguas Frescas, the home of the Almaviva family in The Barber of Seville *and* The Marriage of Figaro. *The set is reminiscent of a Fragonard pastorale. Cherubino appears, dressed as a shepherd. He is in his teens.)*

ROSINA

Cherubino?. . . Cherubino?. . . Cherubino?

(He touches her. She removes her blindfold.)

DUET

ROSINA

Where are you taking me, young shepherd?

CHERUBINO

Look at the green here in the glade.
Feel the mild breeze and the scent of wild thyme.
Hear the vixen's shrill cry and the lamb's complaint.
We're in the Garden of Earthly Delights.

ROSINA

I'm not acquainted with these parts.
I'm lost in this land and frightened.

CHERUBINO

To the north is the Village of Shy Glances.

ROSINA

My soul is closed to sweet pleasures.

CHERUBINO

To the east is the Grove of Tender Touching.

ROSINA

Rage, bitterness, and hate consume me.

CHERUBINO

To the west is the River of Sighs.

ROSINA

Oh, Cherubino, take me home.
I am unworthy of paradise.

CHERUBINO

And south, past the arching willow,
Is the Temple of Love.

Come now, my darling, come with me,
Come to the room I have made for thee.
Let us strew the bed with flowers—
There we will spend the hours.

(Rosina turns to Cherubino and relents.)

ROSINA

Yes, yes, my darling, I'll come with thee,
Come to the room that is made for me.
Let us strew the bed with flowers—
There we will spend the hours.

(Beaumarchais moves closer to Marie Antoinette, who is listening entranced. Louis grows increasingly uncomfortable as Beaumarchais and Marie Antoinette become more intimate.)

QUARTET

BEAUMARCHAIS

Look at the green here in the glade.
Feel the mild breeze and the scent of
    wild thyme.
Hear the vixen's shrill cry and the
    lamb's complaint.
We're in the Garden of Earthly
    Delights.

ROSINA & CHERUBINO
Though hours pass
swiftly, Love is eternal.

BEAUMARCHAIS

To the north is the Village of Shy Glances.

MARIE ANTOINETTE

My soul is closed to sweet pleasures.

BEAUMARCHAIS

To the east is the Grove of Tender Touching.

MARIE ANTOINETTE

Rage, bitterness, and hate consume me.

BEAUMARCHAIS

To the west is the River of Sighs.

MARIE ANTOINETTE

Oh, Beaumarchais, let me be. I am unworthy of paradise.

BEAUMARCHAIS

And south, past the arching willow,
Is the Temple of Love.

BEAUMARCHAIS	MARIE ANTOINETTE	ROSINA & CHERUBINO
Come now, my darling, come with me,	Yes, yes, my darling, I'll come with thee,	The birds are hushed.
Come to the room I have made for thee.	Come to the room that is made for me.	Your cheeks are flushed. The earth is sweet and soft,
Let us strew the bed with flowers—	Let us strew the bed with flowers—	Cool and safe. There we will spend the hours.
There we will spend the hours.	There we will spend the hours.	

(Rosina and Cherubino kiss. Inspired by their example, Marie Antoinette and Beaumarchais move toward each other, but Louis intervenes by placing his sword between their lips.)

LOUIS

No.

SCENE 4

LOUIS

I've had enough.
(The image on the little stage goes to black. The curtain closes.)
I see what's happening here. You want to steal my wife. He wants to steal my wife.
(Brandishing sword at Beaumarchais)
You've written an opera to steal my wife.

BEAUMARCHAIS

I've written an opera to amuse Antonia.

LOUIS

Antonia! Now it's Antonia! Have your arrogance and presumption no limits? Defend yourself if you are a man!

MARIE ANTOINETTE

(To Woman with Hat)
I am frightened.

WOMAN WITH HAT

How exciting! They're fighting over you.

BEAUMARCHAIS

(To Louis, drawing his sword)
With pleasure!

LOUIS

En garde, Beaumarchais.

(Much to the delight of the other ghosts, Beaumarchais and Louis duel. They are both fine swordsmen, but Louis's skills are hampered by excessive posing. The match starts slowly but accelerates and retards, in time with the dueling song.)

DUELING SONG

GHOST QUARTET
He will cut you into pieces.
He will slice you for the pot.
There's another of his caprices.
That's how men do the gavotte.

He will feed him to the dogs.
He's not good enough for hogs.

He's consumed with a raging fire.
Thrust it deeper, get him, Sire!

He will stop him.
He will chop him.
(Etc.)

(Louis drops his sword.)

MARIE ANTOINETTE
Watch out, Louis!

(He regains it.)

OTHER GHOSTS
Louis.

BEAUMARCHAIS
Do you love me, Antonia?

OTHER GHOSTS
Antonia.

BEAUMARCHAIS
Say yes, Your Majesty!

OTHER GHOSTS
Yes.

(Louis runs Beaumarchais through and walks off triumphantly, leaving the sword in him. Marie Antoinette shrieks in horror. Calmly, painlessly, slowly, Beaumarchais pulls the sword out of himself and, kneeling in mock respect, returns it to Louis.)

BEAUMARCHAIS
You forgot your sword, Your Majesty.
(Marie Antoinette bursts out laughing.)
She's laughing!

(The ghosts join in the laughter.)

MARIE ANTOINETTE
We're dead!

BEAUMARCHAIS
You're laughing!

MARIE ANTOINETTE
We're dead!

(Beaumarchais gleefully runs Louis through. Pulling the sword out of his own belly, the king finally joins in the laughter. The scene ends with everyone laughing

and stabbing each other. Over cries of "We're dead," the ghost quartet resumes the dueling song.)

GHOST QUARTET

He will cut you into pieces.
He will slice you for the pot.
There's another of his caprices.
That's how men do the gavotte. . .

(Beaumarchais opens the curtains of the little stage.)

SCENE 5

(The little stage, which had expanded for Scene 3, has now grown even larger. We are at a gala reception in the embassy of the Sublime Porte. The decor pays homage to the Turkomania of Europe in the eighteenth and early nineteenth centuries.

Presiding over a glittering court of officials, harem girls, and Europeans is Suleyman Pasha, a huge, round, jolly man sporting a turban and an embroidered coat. He is seated cross-legged on a cushion placed on a huge Oriental rug. Two large, muscular, oiled bald men, stripped to the waist and wearing baggy pants, are dueling with long, heavy scimitars.

Standing to the side, on a balcony overlooking the street, to the right of an enormous potted palm, are Almaviva, Rosina, and Susanna. The Count anxiously surveys the room. To the left of the tree, partially hidden by the fronds, are Florestine and Léon. Every time the Count looks in their direction, Léon ducks behind the palm, prodded by Florestine. Sometimes she smiles at her father and fans herself rapidly when he looks her way.

The ghosts rush over to watch the action on the little stage, their own duels now forgotten. At the end of their routine the Turkish duelists bow, applauded by the ghosts and the guests, and then exit through a curtained doorway.)

PASHA

(Standing, greeting guests in Turkish)
Selamünaleyküm. [Welcome.] I am Suleyman Pasha. I bid you welcome to my humble abode. Haydi bakalım gelecek oyun başlasın! [Let the next act begin!]

(The Pasha claps his hands. The performers' curtain is raised and several dancers emerge. The Pasha sits.)

LOUIS

(To Beaumarchais)
I can't stay angry with you, you old magician.

MARIE ANTOINETTE

I feel tipsy.

(She giggles.)

LEON

(Peeking out from behind the palm)
Say it, darling, say it!

FLORESTINE
(Seeing Almaviva turning toward her and Léon)
Quick, Léon, hide!
(Léon hides.)

ALMAVIVA
(Turning)
Oh, where is he? The Ambassador is late.
(He turns away.)

LEON
(Looking out)
I don't care about your father. Say it, I beg you.
(As Almaviva turns toward them, Florestine pushes Léon back behind the tree.)

FLORESTINE
Quickly, dearest!

ROSINA
Listen to reason: do not sell the jewels tonight.

ALMAVIVA
My mind is made up.

SUSANNA
But, Master. . .
(Rosina, Almaviva, and Susanna turn away again from Léon and Florestine.)

LEON
(Reappearing)
I no longer know who I am or what I'm doing. One moment I'm on fire, the next I'm like ice. Say it, darling: do you love me?

FLORESTINE
(Tapping head to indicate that Léon is mad)
Poor lad.

MARQUIS
(To Beaumarchais)
She loves you.

LEON
Awake I think of you. Asleep I think of you. Walking, running, reading, eating, breathing, I think of you.

FLORESTINE
Oh, why do I love such a silly, useless boy?

LEON
(With wonder)
She loves me! You love me! Say it again!

FLORESTINE
Not now, my pet. Oh, where is Figaro? He said he'd be here.

BEAUMARCHAIS
(To himself with wonder)
She loves me. . .

MARIE ANTOINETTE
(Silencing Beaumarchais)
Shhh! I'm listening.

(Rosina, Almaviva, and Susanna turn around. Léon hides as Florestine smiles and waves her handkerchief at the Count.)

SUSANNA

Listen to Figaro.

LEON

(Popping head out)
That man is a saint.

(Florestine pushes him back.)

(Bégearss, Wilhelm, and a goon squad of revolutionary guards, thinly disguised as diplomats, enter from a far door.)

ALMAVIVA

That traitor.

LEON

Swear it. Swear you won't marry Bégearss.

SUSANNA

Bégearss is the traitor.

FLORESTINE

(Pushing him back)
The monster. . .

BEGEARSS

(To guards while walking)
. . . but remember, you are foreign diplomats. . .
(Guards nod.)

ALMAVIVA

That man is a saint. . .

FLORESTINE

. . . I'll never marry him.

ALMAVIVA

. . .and my daughter's fiancé.
(He turns his back to Léon and Florestine.)

BEGEARSS

If anyone talks to you, pretend you don't understand.
(The guards nod vigorously.)

LEON

(Reappearing, whispering)
Say it again!

FLORESTINE

(Seeing Bégearss)
Quick, hide!
(Léon does so.)

BEGEARSS

And when he gives him the jewels, then, and not before, you attack like wild dogs and hold the Count in your jaws.

ALMAVIVA

(Seeing Bégearss)
Ah, Bégearss, my friend.

BEGEARSS

(Approaching)
My old friend.

(The page stamps his cane on the floor and rings the bell. The dance music ends.)

PAGE

His Excellency, the British ambassador.

(The onstage musicians scurry together to play an Eastern version of "God Save the Queen." Beaumarchais looks askance at them. The Ambassador is less and less happy with the rendition as it progresses, but the Pasha beams like a proud father at the skill of his musicians. At the end of the anthem the Ambassador bows to the Pasha and joins Almaviva's group. The dancers exit through the performers' curtain and are replaced by acrobats.)

AMBASSADOR

My dear Almaviva, it has been a long time.

ALMAVIVA

We have so much *news* to exchange.
(To Rosina)
You will excuse us, Madam.

(Almaviva and the Ambassador walk off arm in arm, unaware that they are being followed by Susanna, Léon, Florestine, Rosina, Bégearss, Wilhelm, and the revolutionary guards. The Pasha notices this procession and, curious, joins the line. The other people on the little stage observe this strange parade. Finally, everyone is silently staring at the Ambassador and Almaviva, who notice nothing. They stand near the palm tree.)

ALMAVIVA

(With exaggerated politeness)
I. . .
(He clears his throat.)
have a little gift for you, Sir.

AMBASSADOR

And I, for you.

ALMAVIVA

(Looking at Ambassador)
Shall we. . .

AMBASSADOR

(Looking at Almaviva)
Shall we. . .?

(Just as they are about to make the exchange, the Pasha sneezes. The Ambassador and Almaviva look down the line of pursuers to a very embarrassed Pasha, then simultaneously remove their hands from their pockets. During this interaction the other principals look back and forth between the Pasha, on one side, and Ambassador and Almaviva, on the other, as if they were at a tennis match.)

BEGEARSS

Damn!

(The Pasha, giggling, motions for the page to ring his bell.)

PASHA

(Formally)

O excellent ones! O noble gathering! To the singing of Samira, attend! The fragrance of jasmine, the warmth of the desert, the beauty of the moon—Samira!

(The performers' curtain parts and Samira enters, garbed elaborately as an Egyptian singer. During the first part of her aria, an onstage violist, dressed as an Arab musician, performs, seated on a cushion. The Pasha places himself between Almaviva and the Ambassador.)

CAVATINA

SAMIRA

I am in a valley and you are in a valley.
I have no she- or he-camel in it.
In every house there is a cesspool.
That's life.

He beat me then wept, stole my water and then complained.
Some days it's honey, some days onions.
But repetition will teach even a donkey.
That's life.

PASHA

Çok yaşa yavrum! [Long live my baby!]

SAMIRA

Far from the eye, far from the heart.
Keep away from evil and sing to it.

PASHA

Söyle, güzelim! [Sing, my beauty!]

SAMIRA

(Seductively, to Pasha, in Arabic)
Ya habibi, [My love,]
Ya oomri, [My life,]

CABALETTA

Limatha hajartani? [Why did you leave me?]
Hattamta kalbi.[You broke my heart.]
Kayfa tefaloo biya hatha? [How could you do that to me?]
Ya rohi, habaitak, [My soul, I loved you,]
Laken tansa woo-oo-dak. [But you broke all your promises.]

(Samira goes to the performers' curtain, which is now closed. She reaches through its center opening and gracefully pulls out the hand of a beautiful dancing girl, who enters pulling the hand of another girl through the curtain. The sixth

of these sumptuously clothed dancers is Figaro in disguise. He sings and dances with the girls.)

SAMIRA (continued)

Limatha hajartani?
Hattamta kalbi.
(The girls form a line behind Samira and dance to her singing.)
Kayfa tafal biya hatha?
Ya rohi, habaitak,
Laken tansa woo-oo-dak?. . .

(The dancing girls and Figaro echo Samira.)

DANCING GIRLS & FIGARO

Khain! [Traitor!]

SAMIRA

Ya habibi. Ya oomri.

(The singing and dancing grow wilder and wilder. At the end of her number Samira and the group freeze. After the applause, she leaves. The other dancers, including Figaro, bow their heads and then leave the playing area to offer the guests fruit from large bowls.)

DANCING GIRLS

Tafaddaloo marhabun bikoom. . .[Please have some.]

(Almaviva and the Ambassador again try to sneak off together; once again the principals, minus the Pasha, follow them. Figaro makes his way to the head of the line of followers, offering each one in turn some fruit.)

FIGARO

Marhaben bikoom. . .marhaben bikoom. . .

(Almaviva and the Ambassador reach the palm trees. Thinking they are alone, they again start to exchange the money and the diamonds. The girls silently continue to serve the guests.)

ALMAVIVA & AMBASSADOR

Shall we?. . .

(Each puts his hand in his pocket, as Figaro slips between them with his bowl of fruit. With a sexy smile and a wiggle he offers them figs.)

FIGARO

Tafaddaloo marhaben bikoom al figi?

AMBASSADOR

No thank you, Madam.

FIGARO

Figi, figi?

ALMAVIVA & AMBASSADOR

(Aside)
She's offensive.

FIGARO
(Overhearing them, aside, gleefully)
I'm offensive.
(In the guise of being seductive Figaro searches Almaviva's pockets. He thrusts
an orange at Almaviva.)
Tafaddaloo marhaben bikoom al orangy?

ALMAVIVA
(Slapping Figaro's roving hand)
I beg your pardon, Madam.

FIGARO
Orangy?

ALMAVIVA & AMBASSADOR
(Aside)
She's repulsive.

FIGARO
(Aside)
I'm repulsive.

BEGEARSS
(Stepping forward)
Will you please go, Madam?

FIGARO
(Throwing a large avocado at Bégearss)
Avocadi? Avocadi?

ALMAVIVA, AMBASSADOR, BEGEARSS
(Aside)
She's loathsome.

FIGARO
(Frantically searching Almaviva, aside)
I'm loathsome.
(Figaro accidentally tickles Almaviva.)

ALMAVIVA
What are you doing?. . . NOW STOP THAT!

FIGARO
(At his sexiest)
Tafaddaloo marhaben bikoom al banan?

(Leering, he pulls out a banana and thrusts it at Almaviva, while removing the
jewels from his pocket. But Wilhelm has witnessed the theft.)

WILHELM
The jewels! She's got the jewels! Arrest that woman!

MARIE ANTOINETTE
My diamonds!

BEGEARSS
Arrest her!

(Almaviva tries to snatch the jewels back from Figaro, but pulls off his wig instead.)

ALL

Ha! There's Figaro!

FIGARO

(Breaking away from Almaviva)
Oh, no. Not again!

(Figaro begins the chase.)

PURSUERS

Stop!

REVOLUTIONARY GUARDS

(Blocking door)
He stole the jewels!

PURSUERS

Stop!

(Figaro races past Bégearss.)

BEGEARSS

You thief, my plan is shattered!

(Wilhelm appears behind Figaro.)

WILHELM

You'll pay!

ALMAVIVA

You'll pay, you'll pay, you'll pay. . .

PURSUERS

Stop! Stop, Figaro!

(Heavily armed bald Turks with scimitars pursue Figaro.)

TURKS

Ödiyecen!. . . Ödiyecen. . . Ödiyecen!. . . [You'll pay!]

PURSUERS

Stop! Stop! Stop, Figaro!

MARIE ANTOINETTE

(Clapping and shouting)
Bravo, Beaumarchais! It's wonderful!

PURSUERS

Stop! Stop, Figaro!

GHOSTS

Dead!. . . Egg!. . . Bored!. . . Rug!. . . Potato! . . .

(The pursuers ad lib shouts. Figaro hides behind the palm.)

PURSUERS

Where are you, Figaro? Come to me, Figaro!

(Figaro can't resist poking his head out.)

FIGARO

They love me!

PURSUERS

Stop!

FIGARO

Just listen to them!

PURSUERS

Stop, Figaro!

FIGARO

Adorable.

PURSUERS

There is my Figaro. Come to me, Figaro.

FIGARO

What passion!

PURSUERS

Stop!

FIGARO

It's marvelous!

PURSUERS	FIGARO	GHOSTS
Stop, Figaro. . .Stop!	Here's Figaro, your Fi-	Figaro's where?
Stop, Figaro! Stop!	garo.	Figaro's there!
Stop! Stop, Figaro		Figaro here?
Stop! Stop, Figaro!		Figaro's near!
Stop! Stop! Stop!		Figaro's fast!
		Figaro's past!
		Figaro's gone!
		Figaro, Figaro, Figaro. . .

(Figaro races toward the performers' curtain and yanks it open. A band of rheita* players, waiting behind the curtain to make their entrance, mistakenly parades in, blocking Figaro's pursuers. Stunned by the intrusion, they all freeze in position, then resume their chase. The "rheita" players march around the stage, providing Figaro with a constantly moving barrier from his foes.)

PURSUERS

Stop! Stop! Stop, Figaro! Stop! Stop! Stop! Stop, Figaro!

FLORESTINE, SUSANNA, ROSINA,LEON

Go, Figaro, go! Figaro!

PURSUERS

No! No! Stop, Figaro!

GHOSTS

(Ad lib.)
Hurry, Figaro!. . .
Stop them!. . . Go,
Figaro!. . .

---

*   The rheita is an oboe-like North African instrument. The players should actually use disguised ka-zoos.

FLORESTINE, etc.

Fly, Figaro, fly!

PURSUERS	FLORESTINE, etc.	GHOSTS
No, no, my Figaro!	*(Ad lib.)*	Dead. . . Egg. . . Bored. . .
(Ad lib.)	Go, Figaro Figaro!. . .	Rug. . . Potato. . .
There he is!. . . Get	Look out!. . . On your	**THREE CHATTERING**
'im!. . . Over here!. . .	left!. . .	**WOMEN**

Look at Figaro.

(They laugh.)

WOMAN WITH HAT

This is not opera!! Wagner is opera!!

(Figaro runs past the palm toward the balcony. His friends and the "rheita" players hold back the pursuers. The Pasha frantically signals to the page to ring the bell.)

FLORESTINE, etc.

Go, Figaro!

PURSUERS

No! No! Stop, Figaro!. . . No, no, my Figaro!

PASHA	FLORESTINE, etc.
Haydi bakalım gelecek oyun başlasın!	Fly, Figaro, fly! Figaro!

MARIE ANTOINETTE

(Shouting)
I love it! I love it!

(Marie Antoinette, the Marquis, and Louis cheer till the end of act.)

PURSUERS	FLORESTINE, etc.	FIGARO	WOMAN WITH HAT
Stop!. . . Stop!	Go!. . . Go!. . .	*(Standing on bal-cony)*	This is not opera!
Stop!. . .*(Etc.)*	Go!. . .*(etc.)*	I'm home!. . . I'm	Wagner is opera!
THREE		home!. . . I'm	**GHOSTS**
CHATTERING		home!. . .	Dead. . .
WOMEN			Egg. . . Bored. . .
Look at Figaro!			Rug. . . Potato. .

(Cornered, Figaro turns and leaps off the balcony to freedom. The lights black out in mid-leap.)

End of Act I

ACT II

SCENE 1

(Beaumarchais is trying to begin Act II of his opera, but the ghosts are dawdling over intermission. They slowly return to their seats, carrying glasses of wine and chatting animatedly about the opera. One of the ghosts hovers above the stage and then descends into his or her seat.)

BEAUMARCHAIS

Hurry! . . . Hurry! . . . It's late! . . . Madam. . . Sir. . . Hurry! Hurry!. . . The second act is beginning!

LOUIS

(Laughing, to Marie Antoinette)
No, no, no, my dear!

MARIE ANTOINETTE

Of course, he's serious.

LOUIS

It's just an amusement.

MARIE ANTOINETTE

I'll ask him. Beaumarchais, are you claiming that you can bring me back to life?

BEAUMARCHAIS

I can change history.

MARIE ANTOINETTE

(To Louis)
You see?

LOUIS

Abracadabra.

(The curtains of the little stage open onto Figaro's and Susanna's bedroom. It is the following morning. Almaviva, Rosina, Florestine, and Susanna are present.)

ALMAVIVA

I've waited long enough. Figaro won't return the jewels.

MARQUIS

(Mocking)
He will change history.

SUSANNA

My husband is an honest man.

FLORESTINE

And Bégearss is—

ALMAVIVA

I won't listen to your lies. Somehow I'll save the queen.

BEAUMARCHAIS

My words have power.

ALMAVIVA

I have the power.

BEAUMARCHAIS

My music has power.

WOMAN WITH HAT

(Mocking)
Power!

ALMAVIVA

You'll see.

BEAUMARCHAIS

You'll live again, Antonia.

MARIE ANTOINETTE

You think you're God.

ROSINA

He thinks he's God.

MARIE ANTOINETTE

(To Beaumarchais)
It's dangerous to change history.

LOUIS

It's only an opera.

FLORESTINE

Forever scheming.

MARIE ANTOINETTE

You risk your immortal soul.

LOUIS

(To Marquis)
She's dotty.

BEAUMARCHAIS

(To Marie Antoinette)
I don't care about my soul.

SUSANNA

Forever plotting.

MARIE ANTOINETTE

You know the rules. If you change the past you may be caught here forever.

ROSINA, SUSANNA, FLORESTINE
Forever.

(Almaviva paces impatiently.)

BEAUMARCHAIS
(To Marie Antoinette)
I want to make you happy.

MARIE ANTOINETTE
I want to live again. Can you do that, Beaumarchais?

BEAUMARCHAIS
Yes! We shall live in Philadelphia.

ALMAVIVA
(To Susanna)
Well?

LOUIS
If you call that living.

WOMAN WITH HAT
Every day I thank God I'm dead.

ROSINA
(To Susanna)
It's late.

MARIE ANTOINETTE
You don't understand. None of you was ever truly alive. I loved life! I did! I want to live again!

LOUIS
Excessive in life, excessive in death.

(The ghosts laugh.)

FLORESTINE
I'm worried.

MARIE ANTOINETTE
(To Beaumarchais)
I believe you.

BEAUMARCHAIS
At last.

ALMAVIVA
(To Susanna)
Well, where is that husband of yours?

BEAUMARCHAIS
Watch. Now Figaro comes back.

(Figaro enters. He looks disheveled.)

LOUIS

Finally.

ALMAVIVA

Finally.

BEAUMARCHAIS

Listen.

SUSANNA

Where have you been?

FIGARO

All over. I was followed.

BEAUMARCHAIS

(To Marie Antoinette)
Figaro returns the necklace, and then he and the Count rescue you from prison.

ALMAVIVA

Just give me the necklace.

FIGARO

I was thinking—

BEAUMARCHAIS

What?

ALMAVIVA

The necklace.

FIGARO

—about that necklace.
(He takes it out of his pocket.)

BEAUMARCHAIS

The idiot hasn't learned his lines.

SUSANNA

Just give it to him.
(Figaro toys with the necklace and paces. Almaviva follows him.)

BEAUMARCHAIS

(To Figaro)
Just give it to him!

FIGARO

I said to myself, why does my Master want it?

BEAUMARCHAIS

How dare he improvise? Singers have no minds.

ALMAVIVA

To save the queen, idiot.

FIGARO

Why save her?

BEAUMARCHAIS

Why save her?

LOUIS

I love it!

FIGARO

She's spoiled, arrogant, decadent.

BEAUMARCHAIS & MARIE ANTOINETTE

What?

LOUIS

What an idea!

SUSANNA

Figaro!

FIGARO

And a traitor to France.

MARIE ANTOINETTE

I am innocent.

LOUIS

Figaro rebels against Beaumarchais.

FIGARO

Save your family instead.
(*Almaviva lunges for the jewels. Figaro dodges him.*)

BEAUMARCHAIS

Those are not my words.

LOUIS

A theatrical revolution!

MARIE ANTOINETTE

Why are you doing this to me?

ALMAVIVA

I'll kill him!

BEAUMARCHAIS

(*Yelling at the stage*)
I'll kill him!

LOUIS

Brilliant!

WOMAN WITH HAT & MARQUIS

(Applauding)
Bravo!

(The singers cannot hear Beaumarchais.)

FIGARO

She's a vampire, she's a vulture.

BEAUMARCHAIS

(To Figaro)
Viper! Vermin!

MARIE ANTOINETTE

They called me that.

SUSANNA

Listen to me!

FIGARO

What do I care if she loses her head?

LOUIS

He goes too far.

WOMAN WITH HAT

How cruel!

MARQUIS

What fun!

ALMAVIVA

Give me the jewels.

ROSINA, SUSANNA, FLORESTINE

Figaro!

FIGARO

What has the queen ever done for Figaro?

MARIE ANTOINETTE

(To Beaumarchais)
What have I done to deserve this?

ROSINA, SUSANNA, FLORESTINE

Figaro! . . . Figaro, no!

ALMAVIVA

Give me the jewels. . .

ROSINA, SUSANNA, FLORESTINE

Give him the jewels!

FIGARO

Down with Marie Antoinette!
(Everyone gasps.)

FIGARO (continued)
We'll escape to London with the money from the jewels.
(Figaro rushes out. Almaviva is too shocked to pursue him.)

BEAUMARCHAIS
What? Close the curtains!
(The curtains of the little stage close.)

LOUIS
Beaumarchais risk his precious soul? Never. He's just a showman.

MARIE ANTOINETTE
(To Beaumarchais, rising to leave)
I thought you were my friend. But you're like the others. You've hated me all along.

BEAUMARCHAIS
Antonia!

MARIE ANTOINETTE
Thank you for a splendid evening, Monsieur Beaumarchais.

WOMAN WITH HAT
It's just a spoof.

BEAUMARCHAIS
Please don't go, I beg you.

MARIE ANTOINETTE
(Leaving, to Louis)
I shall be at the pavilion.

BEAUMARCHAIS	**GHOSTS**
I'm innocent. . . Please don't go . . . Wait . . . Let me explain. . . It wasn't my idea. . . (Etc.)	Antonia. . . Antonia. . . Antonia. . . Come back! (Etc.)

(Beaumarchais frantically falls to his knees in front of Marie Antoinette, trying to block her exit.)

BEAUMARCHAIS
Wait!
(Marie Antoinette stops.)

ARIA

Figaro was supposed to return the necklace.
The Count was supposed to set you free.
The children were supposed to marry.
The villain was supposed to die.
You were supposed to flee.

I risk my soul for you, Antonia.
Is it all in vain, Antonia,

BEAUMARCHAIS (continued)

All in vain?
(She starts to leave.)

Wait! The Revolution never happens.
There is no guillotine.
A new age dawns.
Poverty is abolished.
Education is free.
A canal in Egypt!
A tower in France!
Balloons deliver mail.
Antonia lives!
(She turns to Beaumarchais.)
I risk my soul for you, Antonia.
Is it all in vain,
All in vain?

(As if in a trance.)

Vast theaters play our visions,
Salons ring with unheard-of sounds.
And there are new fabrics,
Dyed inconceivable colors,
And new kinds of roses, tulips, orchids,
And new industries,
Powered by wind, water, sunlight!
And new sciences—
Mesmerism, magnetism, electricity!
And Antonia lives!
History as it should have been.

MARIE ANTOINETTE

As it should have been.

BEAUMARCHAIS

I do this out of love for you,
All-embracing love for you, Antonia. . .
I will save you.
(During the following exchanges, Beaumarchais journeys from the ghost world into the opera world by walking onstage and passing through the closed curtains.)
I will force Figaro to return the necklace.

MARIE ANTOINETTE

What are you doing?

BEAUMARCHAIS

He will obey me.

MARIE ANTOINETTE

Don't!

LOUIS

Sensational!

BEAUMARCHAIS

The Count will rescue her.

WOMAN WITH HAT

What an effect.

MARIE ANTOINETTE

Stop him!

MARQUIS

A coup de théâtre.

BEAUMARCHAIS

I will enter the opera.

MARIE ANTOINETTE

No!

(The curtains become transparent as Beaumarchais's glowing figure passes through them.)

SCENE 2

(The opera characters, frozen in position, reanimate as the lights come up on them.)

ALMAVIVA

Damn that Figaro!
(To Susanna)
He's *your* husband. You find him.

MARQUIS

(To Woman With Hat)
Well, where's Beaumarchais?

SUSANNA

I don't know where he went.

WOMAN WITH HAT

He's looking for Figaro.

ALMAVIVA

Find him or I'll throw you out.

MARIE ANTOINETTE

It's not Susanna's fault.

SUSANNA

(Bursting into tears)
But, Sir. . .

FLORESTINE	ROSINA	SUSANNA
Father, how could you?	*(To Susanna)*	It wasn't my fault. . . I don't
(To Susanna)	There, there, he doesn't mean	deserve it . . . How could he
There, there.	it.	say that?. . . Why? Why?
(To Almaviva)	*(To Almaviva)*	Why?
It's not her fault.	She doesn't deserve that!	
(To Susanna)	*(To Susanna)*	
Susanna. . .	Susanna. Susanna.	

ALMAVIVA

Enough! I shall not be moved! The queen's life is at stake.
(To Susanna)
I stand by what I said: find Figaro.
(To Rosina and Florestine)
Come, we have to prepare for the ball tonight. It looks as if this will be the last one.

ROSINA

I'll be along in a moment.

(Almaviva and Florestine exit.)

SUSANNA

On my mother's grave—

ROSINA

My dear little Susanna—

SUSANNA

I swear I don't know where he is.

ROSINA

I believe you. My husband is grossly unfair.

SUSANNA

And mine is, too. He gets us both into trouble and then runs away, leaving me to deal with the Count.

ROSINA

Mine was always difficult, but now he's impossible.

SUSANNA

Mine used to be gentle.

ROSINA

Mine used to be loving.

SUSANNA

But what's the use of complaining?

ROSINA

Time changes all.

DUET

SUSANNA

As summer brings a wistful breeze,
Cooling houses, blowing trees,
Women dream their bridal days.

ROSINA

As autumn brings its windy chill
And water freezes on the hill,
Women love and hate their men,
Wishing they were young again.

O time, O time, O thieving time,
Give me back my stolen years.

SUSANNA

As winter brings a longer night,
And women read by candlelight,

SUSANNA & ROSINA

They come to know, like sun, like rain,
Nothing lasts, not love or pain.

O time, O time, O thieving time,
Give me back my stolen years.

ROSINA

And now I must go.

(They embrace.)

SUSANNA

Bless you, Madam, bless you.
(Rosina exits.)
What a kind woman.

(Immediately Figaro enters through the window.)

SUSANNA

Ha!

FIGARO

(Looking over his shoulder)
Quick, hide me!

SUSANNA

Where were you?

FIGARO

I was followed.

SUSANNA

That's what you said the last time.

FIGARO

It's true.

SUSANNA

I don't believe you.
(Beaumarchais suddenly appears behind Figaro.)
Oh, my God, how did he get in?

LOUIS

Oh, there he is.

FIGARO

(Turning around)
That's him!

SUSANNA

It's witchcraft!

FIGARO

(To Beaumarchais)
Who are you, Sir?

BEAUMARCHAIS

(Playing the ghost)
A ghost. Ha-ha-ha. . .!

SUSANNA

I told you.

FIGARO

(Aside to Susanna)
Don't you believe it!
(To Beaumarchais)
I am a ghost, too.
(Imitating Beaumarchais's weird laugh)
Ha-ha-ha. . .!

SUSANNA

Figaro, be careful!

FIGARO

And how, I beg you, Sir Ghost, may I be of service to you?

BEAUMARCHAIS

I demand you return the necklace to your master.

FIGARO

(Aside to Susanna)
He works for the Count.
(To Beaumarchais)
And I demand you crawl back to your hole.

BEAUMARCHAIS

Return the necklace! Save our queen!

SUSANNA

(Timidly)
Who are you, Sir?

BEAUMARCHAIS

I am your creator.

FIGARO

And I am the queen of France.

SUSANNA

(Aside to Figaro)
Do as he says.

BEAUMARCHAIS

Return it!

WOMAN WITH HAT

They don't believe him.
(The ghosts titter.)

FIGARO

Never!

BEAUMARCHAIS

How dare you argue with me? You do not exist.

SUSANNA

I'm frightened.

FIGARO

He's mad.

BEAUMARCHAIS

You are my fantasy.

SUSANNA

Run!

FIGARO

Run!

BEAUMARCHAIS

You can't escape!

MARIE ANTOINETTE

(Calling from ghost world)
Figaro!

BEAUMARCHAIS

Stop!. . .We must save the queen.

FIGARO

You're a stooge for the Count.

MARIE ANTOINETTE

Figaro!

BEAUMARCHAIS

The necklace!

FIGARO
No!

MARIE ANTOINETTE
Figaro!

SUSANNA
Who is that calling?

MARIE ANTOINETTE
Figaro!

BEAUMARCHAIS
(Taking Figaro by the hand)
Come with me.

FIGARO
More tricks.

SUSANNA
Black magic.

FIGARO
No!
(Beaumarchais and Figaro disappear.)

SUSANNA
Where is he?

MARIE ANTOINETTE
Figaro! Figaro!

SUSANNA
Where are they?

MARIE ANTOINETTE
Figaro!

SUSANNA
What is happening?
(Susanna disappears.)

INTERLUDE - "JOURNEY TO LIMBO"

(During this "journey" we see the shadows of Figaro, Susanna, and Beaumarchais slowly moving upward, as if in a dream. Their images occasionally disappear and distort, much like smoke.

At the same time a large scrim descends, which slowly becomes opaque. It serves as a projection screen for the scenery of the Temple of Love, from the Petit Trianon.)

SCENE 3

(Beaumarchais, Susanna, and Figaro enter the ghost world. They move slowly, like somnambulists, looking around in wonder. Marie Antoinette stands in front of the Temple, summoning Figaro.)

MARIE ANTOINETTE

Figaro.

FIGARO

It *is* black magic.

MARIE ANTOINETTE

Approach.

SUSANNA

Don't!

BEAUMARCHAIS

Don't be afraid.

SUSANNA

Be careful!

(Figaro crosses himself and approaches the queen.)

MARIE ANTOINETTE

Figaro.

FIGARO

(To Marie Antoinette, bravely)
Who are you?

MARIE ANTOINETTE

I am your queen.

FIGARO

Impossible. She's on trial this very moment. Why have you brought me here?

MARIE ANTOINETTE

To save my life.

FIGARO

You are an evil spirit.

MARIE ANTOINETTE

Return the necklace.

FIGARO

You are a monster.

MARIE ANTOINETTE

(To Beaumarchais)
Beaumarchais, prove to him I'm innocent. Show him the trial of the queen of France.

(With a gesture Beaumarchais changes the projection to that of the Revolutionary Tribunal, in the Palace of Justice. The enormous hall is lit by only two candles. We can barely see the unruly citizens who have come to enjoy the

spectacle. The ghosts enter, dressed as judges, jury, soldiers, and witnesses. Beaumarchais puts on a wig, assuming the role of the Public Prosecutor. Marie Antoinette plays herself.)

<table>
<tr><td>WOMEN</td><td>CITIZENS</td></tr>
</table>

WOMEN	CITIZENS
Antoinette, we want your head!	Long live the republic!. . . Down with
Antoinette, we want your head!	the monarchy!. . . Kill the aristocrats!. . .

BEAUMARCHAIS

Order!. . .
(The court is quiet.)
Behold: a woman who formerly possessed all the glory that the pomp of kings could invent now occupies the tribunal. Let no one say she did not reap the benefits of the people's justice.

CITIZENS

Hang her royal neck!. . . To the scaffold with her!. . . Look at her now!. . . You reap what you sow!

(Whistles, jeers)

BEAUMARCHAIS

(To Marie Antoinette)
Silence! What is your name?

MARIE ANTOINETTE

Marie Antoinette of Lorraine and Austria, wife of Louis Capet, once king of the French, thirty-eight years of age.

CITIZENS

Kill her!. . . Kill the Austrian! . . .Make her pay with her blood!

BEAUMARCHAIS

Widow Capet, do you think that kings are necessary to the happiness of France?

MARIE ANTOINETTE

That is not for me to decide. My only desire is the happiness of France.

CITIZENS

(Various men)
Make her bleed—that'll make me happy!. . . Give her to me—she can make me happy!. . . Antoinette, you want to make me happy?

BEAUMARCHAIS

Widow Capet, you are charged with squandering enormous sums for your pleasures and intrigues. . .

MARIE ANTOINETTE

I spent more than I wished. Let the truth come to light, I—

BEAUMARCHAIS

(Cutting her off)
and committing treason with your brother the emperor of Austria.

MARIE ANTOINETTE

No! I loved my husband! I loved France!

WOMEN
A-chop, chop, chop,
The guillotine is working overtime.
Ka-thump, thump, thump,
The heads are rolling,
Pouring out their rosy wine.

Come, march,
We'll slaughter the haughty witch.
Join us,
We'll butcher the bitch. . .

BEAUMARCHAIS
You are responsible for the outbreak
of the war.

MARIE ANTOINETTE
I tried to bring peace.

BEAUMARCHAIS
You tried to corrupt and intoxicate the
regiment of Flanders.

MARIE ANTOINETTE
No!

CITIZEN 1
She got me drunk.

CITIZEN 2
She gave feasts and orgies.

MARIE ANTOINETTE
Lies! . . . Lies! . . . Lies! . . .

CITIZEN 3
She slept with everyone.

OTHERS
Whore! . . . Slut . . . Adulteress! . . .

(Laughter, jeers, catcalls.)

BEAUMARCHAIS
(Bangs the floor with his staff)
And finally, there is no doubt that there has been an act of incest between you
and your son, seven years old.

(Marie Antoinette does not reply. A beat of total silence.)

FIGARO
Stop! Leave her alone!

BEAUMARCHAIS
The accused does not reply.

MARIE ANTOINETTE
If I did not reply it was because my nature cannot answer such a charge.
(She stands and turns to the citizens.)
I appeal to all mothers in the courtroom!

WITNESS 1
She had a packet of hair of different colors.

MARIE ANTOINETTE
They come from my dead and living children and from my husband.

WITNESS 2
And a paper with ciphers on it.

MARIE ANTOINETTE

I was teaching my son to count.

WITNESS 3

A gold ring. . .

WITNESS 4

A looking glass . . .

WITNESS 5

A portrait of a woman.

MARIE ANTOINETTE

My mother.

CITIZENS	WOMEN
(Mocking her) Ma-ma. . . ma-ma. . .	Antoinette, we want your head!
Her mother was a cow— moo. . .	Antoinette, we want your head!
moo. . .	Antoinette, we want your head!

(They also imitate dogs, pigs, goats, and birds. Jeers, laughter.)

BEAUMARCHAIS

(Banging staff)
Widow Capet, you are the declared enemy of the French nation. Do you have anything to say in your defense?

MARIE ANTOINETTE

The accusations are un—

BEAUMARCHAIS

(Banging staff)
Silence, bloodsucker! What is the decision of the people of France?

JURY

Yes, to all questions.

FIGARO

No! No! Unjust! This trial is unfair! Set her free!

JURY

(Ignoring Figaro)
In accordance with the first article of the first section of the first chapter of the second part of the penal code, the accused shall be condemned to death.

BEAUMARCHAIS

(To Marie Antoinette)
Have you anything to say?

(Beat of silence as Marie Antoinette realizes that there is no way she can escape death.)

MARIE ANTOINETTE

Nothing.

(Figaro kneels before her.)

FIGARO

Forgive me. I will save you.

(Marie Antoinette ignores him. Susanna crosses herself.)

BEAUMARCHAIS

Today a great example is given to the universe. Nature and reason are satisfied at last. Equality is triumphant with respect to the Widow Capet.

SCENE 4

(This scene crossfades with the previous one. The stage is transformed into an active Paris street. Immediately, a parade of ferocious, unkempt revolutionary women, carrying severed heads on pikes, marches onstage. A ragtag band of street musicians enters with them. The people on the street stop their activities to watch the women. There are vendors of all sorts, strollers, people hanging out of windows. On a makeshift platform, Punch and Judy actors performing before a crowd of children stop their work to watch the frightening parade. The children hide behind their parents.)

WOMEN

A-chop, chop, chop,
The guillotine is working overtime.
Ka-thump, thump, thump,
The heads are rolling,
Pouring out their rosy wine.

Come, march,
We'll slaughter the haughty witch.
Join us,
We'll butcher the bitch.

Antoinette, we want your head!
Antoinette, we want your head!
Antoinette, we want your head!. . .

(Enter Bégearss, leading Wilhelm. They mount the platform, which is immediately vacated by the performers. The children flee. Bégearss silences the women with a gesture.)

BEGEARSS

(To Wilhelm)
Monarchy. Revolution. It's all the same to me. Belief is for fools. I merely lust to rule. I will bend these women to my will. Watch them squirm with delight as I whip them into a frenzy. They want to hate. They need to hate. They will hate! Ah!
(To women)
Women of Paris!

WOMEN

Bégearss! Bégearss! Bégearss!

(Three women come forward with their pikes.)

FIRST WOMAN

We brought you some gifts, sweetie.

(She raises the pike to Bégearss' face.)

SECOND WOMAN

Kiss her lovely lips.

(He kisses the lips of the head.)

THIRD WOMAN

And don't forget to bow. She's a duchess.

SUSANNA

(Aside to Figaro)
God help us.

ARIA WITH CHORUS

BEGEARSS

Women of Paris!
Listen!
Hear!
Listen to their little feet!
Hear them scurry from the corners.
Listen!
Hear!
They are coming to spread their plague.
They assemble in secret cabals.
They whisper in private rooms against us.
They slyly creep down dark streets.
Their shiny fur is pressed against the wall.
They are trying to be invisible,
But we see them.
We see their greedy eyes and hungry mouths.
They want to free the Queen of Rats.
They want to release her from her trap.
But we have her by the tail.
Shall we let her go?

WOMEN

No!

BEGEARSS

Shall we let her go?

WOMEN

Antoinette, we want your head!
Antoinette, we want your head!
Antoinette, we want your head!
Antoinette, we want your head!

A-chop, chop, chop,
The guillotine is working overtime.
Ka-thump, thump, thump,
The heads are rolling,
Pouring out their rosy wine.

Come, march,

WOMEN (continued)

We'll slaughter the haughty witch.
Join us,
We'll butcher the bitch.

Antoinette, we want your head!
Antoinette, we want your head!

BEGEARSS

Listen!
Hear!
The chief rat Almaviva has summoned his rat troops for a rat meeting in his rat
    hole.
They are there right now,
Sharpening their fangs and claws.
What do we do when rats infest our houses?

WOMEN

Exterminate them!

BEGEARSS

What do we do when rats eat our food?

WOMEN

Exterminate them!

BEGEARSS

What do we do when rats rule us?

WOMEN

Extermination!

BEGEARSS

The vermin are having a party tonight at Almaviva's house!

WOMEN

Exterminate them!

BEGEARSS

We'll get them then!

WOMEN

Exterminate them!

BEGEARSS

What do you say?

WOMEN

Antoinette, we want your head. . .

(Bégearss, Wilhelm, and the women march off.)

SCENE 5

(The peers of Paris—those who have not fled or been thrown in jail or exe-cuted—assemble for one last time. Liveried servants take their wraps. The aris-tocrats are decked out in prerevolutionary splendor. They are dressed à la victime, *with thin red ribbons around their necks, commemorating relatives and loved ones lost to the guillotine.*

Three ghosts—the gossips—haunt the ball. They are dressed in the same fashion as the guests—but their clothing is all white and their makeup has a waxy pallor. The First and Second Ghosts mingle with the guests; the Third Ghost sits on a chandelier. The ghosts cannot be seen, heard, or touched by the other guests. Rosina and Almaviva stand to one side, greeting people. Nearby, next to a pillar, Florestine paces nervously.)

ROSINA

(To an older woman, embracing her)
Welcome, Madeleine, welcome.

FIRST GHOST

(To Second Ghost)
I knew that woman.

ALMAVIVA

(Kissing the ring of a bishop)
Your excellency, welcome.

FIRST GHOST

(Waving to woman)
Madeleine!

OLDER WOMAN

(To Rosina)
They took Philippe.

(The First Ghost reaches out to the older women but her hand goes through her.)

FIRST GHOST

Aunt Madeleine!. . . Aunt Madeleine!

ROSINA

No one is safe in Paris.

SECOND GHOST

(To First Ghost)
She can't hear you.

BISHOP

(To Almaviva)
They took away my church.

ALMAVIVA

Damn them!

ROSINA

(To another friend)
Diane, I'm glad you could come.

THIRD GHOST

(Waving gaily from chandelier)
Diane!. . . Diane!

(A young man kisses Florestine's hand.)

FLORESTINE

Have you seen Léon?

FIRST YOUNG MAN

No, I'm sorry.

SECOND GHOST

(To First Ghost)
Her young man left her.

BISHOP

And they closed the convent.

(A friend greets Rosina.)

ROSINA

Blanche.

(Rosina and Blanche embrace.)

THIRD GHOST

Marguerite!

FLORESTINE

(To another young man)
Have you seen Léon?

SECOND YOUNG MAN

Not since Easter.

ALMAVIVA

You must leave tomorrow.

ROSINA

They said you went to Brussels.

THIRD GHOST

There's my old friend . . . Joseph!

FLORESTINE

(To a young woman)
Have you seen Léon anywhere?

YOUNG WOMAN

I saw him last week.

FLORESTINE

Father banished him from the house.

ROSINA

What difficult times.

BISHOP

We must never give up hope.

FLORESTINE

I don't know where he is.

(She cries in her friend's arms. The First and Second Ghosts approach her.)

FIRST GHOST

Poor girl.

SECOND GHOST

Poor Florestine.

ALMAVIVA

(To other friends)
Welcome. . .

THIRD GHOST

Julien!

ROSINA

(To another friend)
Good to see you.

FLORESTINE

Where did he go?

ALMAVIVA

So glad to see you. . . Your grace. . .
(He claps for attention, and the musicians stop playing.)
Friends, welcome. For one last time we have come together in the name of love
and amity. But even as I speak, all of France suffers and our queen awaits her
verdict. When I think of her I reproach myself the air I breathe, and am torn between pain and rage. But tonight, let us forget our sorrow and celebrate this moment of freedom. Let the golden days return! Musicians!

*(Everyone dances—even the ghosts—except the Almaviva household. For a mo-
ment all pains are forgotten as the salad days of the monarchy are revived. After
a while Léon enters furtively. He stands partially hidden near Florestine.)*

LEON

(Sotto voce)
Florestine!

FLORESTINE

Léon!
(She embraces him.)

LEON

Your father!

FLORESTINE

I don't care!
(Léon holds her. Almaviva sees them.)

ALMAVIVA

(Pointing out Léon to Rosina)
Your son!

(Almaviva tries to go to Léon, but Rosina restrains him.)

ROSINA

Don't!

FLORESTINE

Thank God you're safe!

ALMAVIVA	LEON

How dare he come here? I'll have him   Darling!
thrown out!

FLORESTINE

I thought you had left me.

LEON

Leave you?

ROSINA

Will you?
(Almaviva attempts to speak but Rosina cuts him off.)
Will you?

FLORESTINE

I was so frightened.

ALMAVIVA

(Aside)
I know she's right. We committed the same sin. . .

ROSINA

(Aside)
What can I do to make him forgive me?

ALMAVIVA

(Aside)
Yet I can't forgive her.

LEON

How could I leave you?

QUARTET

LEON

Remember the chestnut trees
In the gardens of the Tuileries?

FLORESTINE

You took me by the hand.

ALMAVIVA

I'd like to touch her hand.

ROSINA

I wish he'd take my hand.

LEON

Remember the mist on the Seine
And the bridges in the easy rain?

FLORESTINE

You held my face and kissed me.

LEON

I held you. I kissed you.

FLORESTINE

Remember the fallen birch
In the cloister of the little church?

LEON

I took you by the hand.

FLORESTINE

Remember us drifting, afloat,
In the silence of the gliding boat?

LEON

I held your face and kissed you.

FLORESTINE

You shivered and trembled.

ALMAVIVA

Look how she loves him.

LEON

You quivered and sighed.

ROSINA

Look how he loves her.

LEON

Remember the fragrance of mushrooms in the air?

ROSINA

I remember a shimmering light.

ALMAVIVA

I remember a star-filled night.

FLORESTINE

I remember there were raindrops in your hair.

LEON, FLORESTINE

I swore to love you always.
I gave myself to you forever.

ALMAVIVA

I swore to love her always.

ROSINA

I gave myself to him forever.

(Suddenly the doors burst open. Bégearss enters, leading the revolutionary women and the soldiers. The musicians stop playing. The party freezes in position. There is a stunned silence.)

BEGEARSS

I hope I'm not too late for your party. My dear Almaviva, why didn't you invite your old friend Bégearss?

ALMAVIVA

My friend, I don't understand. What is the meaning of this?

BEGEARSS

Citizens, arrest the aristocrats!

(The soldiers seize the guests.)

FIRST GHOST

Let's tell the others.

SECOND GHOST

Let's tell Her Majesty.

(The ghosts disappear.)

BEGEARSS

(To Almaviva)
Now do you understand?

ALMAVIVA

You have betrayed me!

ROSINA

.We are lost!

LEON

Traitor!

FLORESTINE

Judas!

BEGEARSS

The necklace.

ALMAVIVA

I don't have it.

BEGEARSS

Where is it?

ALMAVIVA

I don't know.

BEGEARSS

(Brutally)
Give it to me!. . .
(Sweetly)
Or perhaps you would prefer to talk to my friends here.

(Figaro and Beaumarchais enter and watch unnoticed.)

REVOLUTIONARY WOMEN

Give 'im to me!. . . No, me!

ALMAVIVA

I don't know!

REVOLUTIONARY WOMEN

He doesn't know!

ROSINA & FLORESTINE

He doesn't know!

FIGARO

(Stepping forward and giving Bégearss the necklace)
Stop! *I* have it, you traitor.

BEGEARSS

(Holding diamonds aloft)
At last! I have you, Almaviva. I seize this in the name of the people. It will be used to feed the poor and house the homeless.

(Bégearss puts the necklace in his coat pocket as the revolutionary women cheer and whistle. Susanna enters and hides behind a pillar. From time to time she peeks her head out. The rest of the ghosts, led by Marie Antoinette and Louis, enter.)

ALMAVIVA

Forgive me, Figaro. Once again you have proved me a fool.

BEGEARSS

My hatred is in full bloom. Almaviva, I am now your equal. Now we are *all* aristocrats. And I want to marry Florestine. You will give me your daughter's hand.

ROSINA & LEON

No!

ALMAVIVA

I will never allow it.

BEGEARSS

I want that pleasure.
(Sweetly)
You have the night to reconsider. Deny me and you will all die.
(To Wilhelm)
Take them to prison.

FIGARO

(To Beaumarchais)
Free us. Use your powers.

BEGEARSS

(Whirls around)
Powers? What powers? I have all the power.

BEAUMARCHAIS

(To the soldiers, making a magical gesture)
Release them!

(Nothing happens.)

MARIE ANTOINETTE

(To Louis)
I knew it. He's lost his strength.

LOUIS

He's become mortal.

MARQUIS

Poor man.

BEAUMARCHAIS

(Repeating the gesture)
I command you!
(Nothing happens.)

BEGEARSS

(To Figaro)
Your friend is mad.

BEAUMARCHAIS

I am as weak as smoke.

BEGEARSS

(To Wilhelm)
Take them to prison.
(To Almaviva)
I'll see you at dawn.
(To onstage orchestra)
Musicians, play. Amuse the aristocrats as they go off to their cell.

(Exit Bégearss.)

WILHELM

(To the prisoners)
This way, and be quick about it.

(The guards start to march everyone off, when Susanna comes out from behind the pillar. She has stuffed her shawl under her skirt so that she appears pregnant. She staggers as though she is carrying triplets.)

SUSANNA

(Pointing at Wilhelm and at her belly)
Stop!. . . He did it! He did it!. . . That's the man! Stop!. . . Stop!. . . Get him!

WILHELM

Susanna!. . . I mean, I don't know this woman!. . . I didn't do it!. . . Susanna, don't!

(The revolutionary women and the guards, diverted by Susanna, relax their vigilance for a moment.)

GUARDS, REVOLUTIONARY WOMEN

(Mimicking Susanna)
He did it!. . . That's the man!. . . Susanna!. . . Oh, Wilhelm!

SUSANNA

(Aside to Figaro and Beaumarchais)
Run!. . . This way!. . . Go! . . .

SUSANNA (continued

(To the soldiers)
He did it!. . . That's the man!

(Figaro and Beaumarchais escape in the confusion.)

WILHELM

Stop them!. . . They're escaping!. . . Don't you see?. . . What am I going to do?. . . What am I going to do?. . . Take them away!. . . Master'll kill me!
(Finally realizing that Figaro and Beaumarchais are escaping, the soldiers run off after them, but it's too late. They seize Susanna. To soldiers:)
Take them away!
(Aside)
Oh, he's going to kill me! He'll kill me.

(Wilhelm, the soldiers, revolutionary women, guests, and Almaviva household all leave. The stage is empty, except for the musicians and the ghosts, who start dancing a spectral version of the ball, gracefully exchanging heads and limbs.)

MARIE ANTOINETTE

He sacrificed his powers to bring me back to life. Because he loves me. He loves me.

(The curtains close.)

INTERLUDE

SCENE 6

(The curtains open, revealing the dismal Gothic-vaulted interior of the Conciergerie prison. It is night. Candle and torchlight disclose two levels. On the first is a large barracklike cell containing a group of terrified, disheveled aristocrats awaiting execution. An ancient, demented duchess with grand manners, wearing a decaying extravagant hat and a ball gown, is serving imaginary tea to imaginary guests. She is the living version of the Woman with Hat. Two men are sitting in a corner, quietly talking. Most of the other prisoners are lying on straw pallets, trying to sleep. Stone steps with iron railings lead to a walkway and a second level of smaller cells, the barred doors of which are visible.)

DUCHESS

(Chatting with an imaginary guest)
I am very well, my dear Marquis. Would you like a cup of tea?
(To imaginary servant)
Madeleine, bring Marguerite some chocolate.
(She walks away chatting)
Oo-long lai-chi, from Nanking.

FIRST ARISTOCRAT

(To Second Aristocrat, handing him a letter)

If you should survive tomorrow, please give this to my wife. It is my last request.

(Duchess laughs in reaction to a bitchy remark.)

SECOND ARISTOCRAT

How could I, my friend? No one survives a visit to the guillotine.

DUCHESS

(To another "guest")
She was wearing a gown of red pekin, trimmed with tiny white roses. It was exquisite.
(Reacting to a compliment)
I'm so fond of rubies. Grandmother gave them to me. She lived to a hundred and three, and drank only wine. But say what you will, Diane's trout were divine.
(To a gossip)
Shocking, my dear. With a bishop?

(She laughs. The cell door bangs open. Wilhelm, backed by a group of guards, pushes the Almaviva group into the cell. The Duchess freezes and stares at them, then retreats into the shadows.)

WILHELM

In you go, aristocrats.
(To Rosina, pulling her by the arm)
Here, you stay with me, Countess.

GUARDS

(Jeering)
Countess. . . Countess. . .

(Almaviva pushes Wilhelm away from Rosina and stands between them.)

ALMAVIVA

Don't you touch her!

(Wilhelm is about to strike Almaviva, but the guards restrain him.)

ROSINA & SUSANNA

Leave him alone!

FLORESTINE & LEON

Don't hurt him!

GUARDS

No! No!

WILHELM

Don't worry, I won't harm him. He's a special guest of Citizen Bégearss.
(To Almaviva)
Perhaps he'll invite you to join our gracious queen. She's staying in the royal suite.
(Dangling a large keyring, he points to the second level.)
Upstairs. They say she is leaving for a long voyage in the morning. Sleep well, aristocrats.

(Wilhelm leads the guards off, banging the door shut behind them. The Almaviva group looks around disconsolately. Almaviva sits on a bench near the door, staring at the floor. With a sigh Rosina sits next to him. Florestine and Léon go to another bench nearby. Susanna stands. Silence.)

ROSINA

(To Almaviva)
You were very brave.

FLORESTINE

You could have been hurt.

SUSANNA

(To Florestine)
His only thought was for your mother.
(Still Almaviva does not respond.)

LEON

I am proud of you, Father.
(After a long pause Almaviva looks up at Léon.)

ALMAVIVA

Father? Still you call me that after the way I've treated you? I am so ashamed.
(Léon falls to his knees in front of Almaviva and embraces him.)

ALMAVIVA

(To Rosina)
I beg your forgiveness.

ROSINA

It's I who caused you pain.

ALMAVIVA

I was arrogant and prideful.

ROSINA

I was foolish and vain.

ALMAVIVA

You were lonely.
(Rosina and Almaviva embrace.)
Rosina.

(Léon and Florestine approach Almaviva and Rosina. Susanna joins them. They all embrace each other for a moment.)

QUINTET & MISERERE

ALMAVIVA, ROSINA, FLORESTINE, LEON, SUSANNA

O God of love,
O Lord of light,
Redeeming, embracing Savior,
Thank you for this moment of peace.

Storm and fire overwhelm me,
Fear and death are at my door,
But the thought of these dear faces
Brings me rest in this time of war.

(A candle is lit in one of the cells above, casting the flickering silhouette of a woman on the opposite wall. She is not seen otherwise.)

MARIE ANTOINETTE

Please hear my last prayers that You will receive my soul.

(Almaviva hears Marie Antoinette and looks up.)

ALMAVIVA

(With wonder)
Your Majesty!

(Almaviva runs up the stairs and falls to his knees in front of Marie Antoinette's door.)

Miserere mei, Deus,	[Have mercy on me, O Lord,
secundum magnam misericordiam tuam.	according to Your great mercy.
Dele iniquitatem meam,	Wipe out my iniquity,
et a peccato meo munda me;	and cleanse me from sin;
et peccatum meum contra me est semper,	sin is always before me,
et in peccatis concepit me mater mea.	in sin my mother conceived me.
Incerta et occulta sapientiae tuae manifestasti mihi;	Mysterious and hidden things of Your wisdom you have shown me;
lavabis me, et super nivem dealbabor,	You will wash me, and I will become whiter than snow,
et exsultabunt ossa humiliata.	and my crushed bones will rejoice.
Miserere mei, Deus.	Have mercy on me, Lord. Amen.]
Amen.	

MARIE ANTOINETTE

I ask forgiveness of those I have known for the sorrow I have caused them. I forgive my enemies the evil they have done me. I say farewell to my family and friends. Adieu, adieu.

ALMAVIVA, ROSINA, FLORESTINE, LEON, SUSANNA

O God of love,
O Lord of light,
Redeeming, embracing Savior,
Grant her but a moment of peace.

Storm and fire overwhelm her,
Fear and death are at the door.
Let the thought of her dear faces
Bring her rest in this time of war.

(Marie Antoinette blows out her candle. Almaviva returns to the lower level. The prisoners make themselves as comfortable as possible and go to sleep. On the other side of the barred windows, the sun rises. Susanna awakens with a start as a cock crows. She looks around. Seeing no one, she starts to relax. But the cell door creaks open, and as she watches, two ominous, cloaked figures enter.)

SUSANNA

(Whispering to Rosina)
We are finished.

ROSINA

Farewell, my faithful friend.

FLORESTINE

I'm frightened.
(The other prisoners have awakened.)

LEON

At least we shall die together.

SUSANNA

I wish Figaro were here.

ALMAVIVA

(Holding Rosina)
Stay close to me.
(The figures approach him. One is Figaro.)

FIGARO

(Disguising his voice)
Almaviva, prepare to meet your maker.

ALMAVIVA

(Blustering)
See here, how dare you disturb our sleep? We are the private prisoners of
Citizen Bégearss.
(Figaro makes eerie sounds.)
You can't frighten me. If you don't withdraw immediately I shall be forced to—

FIGARO

(Pulling back his hood)
For God's sake, don't you recognize your old Figaro?

FLORESTINE, ROSINA, SUSANNA

Figaro!

ALMAVIVA

You idiot!

DUCHESS

(To Beaumarchais)
Would you like a cup of tea?

BEAUMARCHAIS

No, thank you.

FIGARO

We've come to lead you to freedom.
(Figaro locks the door and dangles a large key.)

LEON

How did you get it?

FIGARO

Bribery, larceny, and a little violence. But we don't have the key to Her Majesty's cell. Wilhelm has it.

BEAUMARCHAIS

What will we do?

ALMAVIVA

What can we do?

SUSANNA

Wilhelm has it? You men can rest now. Let the women do some work. Come, ladies.

(Susanna, Rosina, and Florestine have a little conference. They laugh and titter as the men descend the stairs.)

LEON

(To Almaviva)
I'm afraid the game is over.

ALMAVIVA

All is lost, dear Figaro.

FIGARO

Not with my Susanna in command.
(The women break for action.)
Just watch.

ROSINA

(Calling through the bars of the cell door)
Oh, Wilhelm! Wilhelm!

ALMAVIVA

Rosina, what are you—

(Rosina puts her hand over his mouth. Wilhelm appears.)

WILHELM

You called, Countess?

(Rosina pretends that she is about to faint.)

ROSINA

Help me, someone, help!

ALMAVIVA

(Aside to Figaro)
She's lost her mind.

SUSANNA

My mistress feels faint.

ROSINA

(Opening her bodice)
I can't breathe!

FLORESTINE

We can't untie the knot.

WILHELM

(Brandishing musket)
No tricks now or you'll regret it.

SUSANNA

For the love of God, please go to her.

SUSANNA (continued)

(The women fall into provocative poses as Wilhelm unlocks the door and enters the cell. To the men, aside)
You men, go hide.

(Almaviva, Léon, Beaumarchais, and Figaro step into the shadows.)

FLORESTINE

Look, her breathing is diminished.

ROSINA

(Opening her bodice some more)
Another second and I'll be finished.

ALMAVIVA

(Aside to Rosina)
Rosina!

BEAUMARCHAIS

(To Figaro)
Your wife is bold but never mannish.

FIGARO

Her dad was Welsh, her mother Spanish.

LEON

Just one mistake, our heads will vanish.

WILHELM

And here I thought that you were clannish.

ROSINA

(Groaning)
Oh, open my bodice.

WILHELM

I won't fall for that.

FLORESTINE

A man like you is heaven sent.

ALMAVIVA

(To Léon)
A wife should be obedient.

LEON

It's just a small divertissement.

BEAUMARCHAIS

(To Figaro)
These women are magnificent.

(The women surround Wilhelm, who realizes that he's in danger.)

WILHELM

Let me out of here!

SUSANNA

(Stroking his face)
Don't be so belligerent.

FLORESTINE

(Stroking his pistol)
What a piece of armament!

WILHELM

No!

ROSINA

(Revealing some leg)
Help!

SUSANNA

(Aside to Florestine)
Look, his face is turning red.

FLORESTINE

At least he isn't dead.

ROSINA

God, take me to your bed!

ALMAVIVA

She's doing it for spite.

LEON

Oh, Father, what a night!

BEAUMARCHAIS

A woman free is man's delight.

FIGARO

What's a bitch without a bite?

SUSANNA

(To Wilhelm, with arms outstretched)
You must come to me!

FLORESTINE

You're so strong.

ROSINA

And such a *man*.
(The women all swoon.)

ALMAVIVA

Oh, Rosina, how can you?

WILHELM

(Seduced)
Do you think so?

ROSINA

(Sultry)
Please!

(Wilhelm goes to touch Rosina's bosom. Without realizing it, he hands his musket to Susanna, who immediately knocks him senseless with it. Dropping the gun, she snatches his keyring and throws it to Almaviva.)

SUSANNA

So much for endless talk.
(To Almaviva)
Free Her Majesty.

(Almaviva runs toward the stairs leading to Marie Antoinette's cell. The queen has lit her candle, casting a silhouette again.)

ALMAVIVA

Your Majesty!

(Bégearss and his men stand at the head of the stairs.)

BEGEARSS

No escape.
(To Almaviva)
My dear Count, you disappoint me. I should have thought you'd realize that your position is hopeless.

WILHELM

(Coming to)
Oh, my aching head. . . What happened?. . . Oh, God!
(Crawling to Almaviva)
Oh, Master, they tricked me again. Oh, Master, will you ever forgive me?

BEGEARSS

(Pleasantly)
Master? Master? My boy, have you forgotten that the Revolution has made us all equal citizens? Of course I forgive you.

(Wilhelm smiles, relieved, and kisses Bégearss' hand.)

WILHELM

Thank you. . . Thank you . . .

BEGEARSS

(Suddenly pulling his hand away, coldly)
But the Revolution does not. You are unfit to serve her.
(To guards, pointing at Wilhelm)

Seize him!

(The guards seize Wilhelm.)

WILHELM

ALMAVIVA	SUSANNA	ROSINA
You traitor!	Monster!	Murderer!

(Whimpering)

No!. . . Please!. . .

BEGEARSS

(To Almaviva)
And now, my friend, about that little matter we discussed earlier: your daughter's hand or death to you and your entire family.

FIGARO

Wait!
(Pointing to Bégearss)
I denounce that man in the name of the Revolution. Search his coat and you will find the queen's necklace. He has kept it for himself.

BEGEARSS

(Laughing)
That's ridiculous. Take him away!

(The guards continue to lead the group off.)

WILHELM

It's true! It's true! He plans to sell it in London.

BEGEARSS

Shut up! He's lying!

(The guards halt and listen to Wilhelm.)

WILHELM

I know all his secrets. He hates the Revolution. All he cares about is himself, and what's more—

BEAUMARCHAIS

They say his mother was a duchess.

DUCHESS

(To Bégearss, trying to embrace him)
Son, my son.

BEGEARSS

(Pushing her away)
Get away from me! Take them away!

(The guards look confused.)

BEAUMARCHAIS	BEGEARSS
He's a counterrevolutionary!	No!. . . No, I'm innocent!

FIGARO

(Catching on to Beaumarchais's plan)
He's a spy for the English.

GUARDS

Spy? He's a spy for the English. . . Spy. . . Spy. . .

FIGARO

Arrest him!

(The guards seize Bégearss as Wilhelm searches him for the necklace.)

BEGEARSS

Let me go!. . . Don't touch me! . . . No! No!

WILHELM

BEGEARSS	GUARDS	FIGARO
No!. . . No!. . . innocent!	Spy!. . .Traitor! Counter-	*(To Wilhelm, taking the*
No!. . . No!. . . (Etc.)	revolutionary!. . .To the guil-	*necklace)*
	lotine. . .The	Here let me see.
	necklace. . .(Etc.)	

WILHELM

(Snatching it back)
It's mine!

BEAUMARCHAIS

(Taking the necklace from Wilhelm)
May I see?

(Holding the necklace aloft)
You see? You see?

DUCHESS

(To Bégearss)
Some tea? Some tea?

(Bégearss struggles with his captors.)

(In the confusion Figaro starts to lead the group out the door and down the corridor.)

FIGARO

This way. . . Hurry!. . . Quickly!. . .

(Almaviva is torn between freeing the queen and leaving with his family. Beaumarchais recognizes his dilemma and takes the keyring from his hand.)

BEAUMARCHAIS

Allow me.

(Almaviva smiles and bows, then continues out. Beaumarchais runs up the stairs.)

BEGEARSS

Fools, they're escaping!

(Standing in the doorway, Figaro ushers the prisoners out the door.)

WILHELM

(Seeing Beaumarchais with the necklace)
My necklace!

GUARDS

Spy!. . . The necklace!. . . Traitor. . . To the guillotine!. . .

BEGEARSS

Get them!

(The guards chase out Figaro and the prisoners, dragging Bégearss and Wilhelm along.)

GUARDS

Stop!

(Figaro waves goodbye to Beaumarchais, who waves back. Figaro exits pursued by the guards.)

Stop!. . . Stop!. . . Stop, Figaro!

(Beaumarchais is left alone on stage.)

BEAUMARCHAIS

Goodbye, Figaro. . . Take care. . . Safe journey. . .

(He sighs.)

You were my favorite child. Goodbye, Figaro. Goodbye, Beaumarchais. You've come to the end of your road. And for the sake of the ghost of a woman who doesn't even love you.

(Quietly)

But I love you, Antonia.

(To door)

Your Majesty, I give you your life. Be ready for freedom! I am opening the door!

(The silhouette of the prisoner queen stands. Beaumarchais puts the key in the lock.)

MARIE ANTOINETTE (GHOST)

(Quietly)

No, Beaumarchais.

(He spins around and sees the ghost of Marie Antoinette.)

BEAUMARCHAIS

Antonia, what are you saying? She must escape for you to live!

(She shakes her head as he tries to convince her.)

Almaviva brings her to London. The Revolution fails! A new age dawns! Antonia lives! History as it should have been!

MARIE ANTOINETTE

No.

ARIA

She must stay
And ride the cart
And see the crowds
And hear the drums
And count the stairs
And feel the blade—
Fear, terror, panic!

She must stay,
Beaumarchais,
And she must die.

Once there was a golden child
Who lived in a garden of silver trees.
Her steps made the earth resound,
Her cries swayed the cathedral spires.

She was the chosen one,
But monsters scaled her garden walls.

They looked like men and kissed her hand,
And brought her gifts from East and West,
But in each smiling face she saw lizard eyes.

MARIE ANTOINETTE (continued)
"Do you love me?" the girl would ask,
Then watch the serpent mouthing, "Yes."
I had to stay,
Beaumarchais,
And I had to die.

But there was no peace.
Bereft of substance,
I wafted like a vapor,
Cold, empty,
Longing for the kingdom and the garden,
And even the monsters—
Until, with your art and love,
You called me.
Luminous and noble,
You wanted me when I had nothing,
And would die again to give me life.

My pride has kept us far apart.
Your warmth now melts my frozen heart.

I love you.

(She kneels before him.)

BEAUMARCHAIS

(Lifting her)
Come, Antonia.

(The figures glow. Beaumarchais gestures and the soldiers appear. They take the prisoner queen away.)

FINALE

(Immediately the walls of the prison rise, revealing the enormous Place de la Révolution. Toward the back of it looms a towering guillotine. On the opposite side of the stage is a gaily painted Montgolfier balloon. Large crowds of Parisians in their Sunday best have come to view the execution of their monarch and the balloon ascent. The gardens of Aguas Frescas appear high up, hazily lit, as if in a vision. Beaumarchais and the ghost Marie Antoinette slowly ascend toward it, arm in arm.

Led like a tethered animal by a cord tied to her hands, the prisoner queen is brought by the soldiers to a shabby cart drawn by two dray horses. To further humiliate her they place her in it so that she is sitting backward. She is wearing a simple white gown and bonnet and is accompanied by the executioner and a revolutionary priest. As the cart slowly makes its way to the guillotine, the crowds shout and chant.)

CROWD

Long live the Republic!. . . Down with tyranny!. . . Death to the Austrian!. . . There's the wicked Antoinette! She's finally finished!. . . Antoinette, we want your head. . . (Etc.)

(At the same time the now forgotten Almaviva household stealthily makes its way to the balloon. When the cart draws up beside the scaffold, the queen, refusing help, alights by herself and quickly mounts the steps. The executioner places her head on the block. Figaro severs the mooring rope of the balloon, which coincides with the fall of the guillotine blade. The crowd roars its approval and, accompanied by an onstage band, sings "La Marseillaise.")

CROWD

Allons enfants de la Patrie
Le jour de gloire est arrivé.
Contre nous de la tyrannie
L'étendard sanglant est levé.
Entendez-vous dans ces campagnes
Mugir ces féroces soldats?
Ils viennent jusque. . .

(The sounds of the crowd and the onstage music slowly fade out, the lights on the Place de la Révolution gradually dim to black, and the balloon rises and disappears.

By now Beaumarchais and the queen have arrived at Aguas Frescas. Louis is waiting there with the other ghosts, holding the Duchess' hand and smiling. An increasingly bright spotlight illuminates Beaumarchais and Marie Antoinette as the lights on Aguas Frescas dim. Finally, only they are illuminated as he places the jewels around her neck and then kisses her hand. Fade to black.)

End of the Opera